OVERCOMING THE SENIOR SLUMP

Meeting the Challenge with Internships

Randall G. Glading

Rowman & Littlefield Education
Lanham • New York • Toronto • Plymouth, UK
2008

Published in the United States of America
by Rowman & Littlefield Education
A division of Rowman & Littlefield Publishers, Inc.
A wholly owned subsidiary of The Rowman & Littlefield Publishing Group, Inc.
4501 Forbes Boulevard, Suite 200, Lanham, Maryland 20706
www.rowmaneducation.com

Estover Road, Plymouth PL6 7PY, United Kingdom

Copyright © 2008 by Randall G. Glading
The appendix and figure 1 are used with permission of the International Center for Leadership in Education (see www.LeaderEd.com).

All rights reserved. No part of this publication may be reproduced, stored in a retrieval system, or transmitted in any form or by any means, electronic, mechanical, photocopying, recording, or otherwise, without the prior permission of the publisher.

British Library Cataloguing in Publication Information Available

Library of Congress Cataloging-in-Publication Data

Glading, Randall G., 1955–
  Overcoming the senior slump : meeting the challenge with internships / Randall G. Glading.
    p. cm.
  Includes bibliographical references.
  ISBN-13: 978-1-57886-770-7 (cloth : alk. paper)
  ISBN-10: 1-57886-770-3 (cloth : alk. paper)
  ISBN-13: 978-1-57886-769-1 (pbk. : alk. paper)
  ISBN-10: 1-57886-769-X (pbk. : alk. paper)
  1. High school seniors—United States. 2. College attendance—United States. 3. College student orientation—United States. 4. High school graduates—Employment—United States. I. Title.
  LB2350.G58 2008
  373.12'27—dc22
                                                            2007045126

∞™ The paper used in this publication meets the minimum requirements of American National Standard for Information Sciences—Permanence of Paper for Printed Library Materials, ANSI/NISO Z39.48-1992.
Manufactured in the United States of America.

CONTENTS

Foreword		v
Bruce S. Cooper		
Acknowledgments		xv
1	Adolescence to Adulthood	1
2	Secondary Education Today	11
3	The Postsecondary Experience	29
4	The Internship Movement	41
5	Nine Stories from the Field	55
6	Student Internships: Shaping the High School Experience	65
7	The Portal to Success and Personal Growth	83
8	The Impact of the Internship Experience on Life beyond College	103
9	Recommendations for Parents, Schools, Students, and Postsecondary Institutions	109

Final Thoughts 137

Appendix: Achieving Academic Excellence through Rigor
  and Relevance 139
  Willard R. Daggett

Bibliography 151

About the Author 157

FOREWORD

We have all seen it, felt it—after about eleven years of plowing ahead, staying up late, reading until our eyes hurt, we are now at last *high school seniors*, able to ratchet down and float since presumably the die is cast. Our record in high school is virtually complete, our grade point average set, and we may even know which college or university, if any, that we are attending next year. This senior slump has become so common that it is almost a disease: "senioritis," "senior goofing off," being cool, and not giving a fig. And what could have been an important final year of learning (what we want to master at a higher level) can turn into a super waste of time. Randall Glading hits the critical nerve in this book: what to do to make the high school senior year meaningful, to help erect and effectively pave the "bridge" between high school senior year, college, and adult life, what Michael Kirst has called the K–16 continuum. For the senior year stands at the door between high school adolescence and college adulthood.

Thus, this book meets a critical need: how best to help our children to move effectively from childhood to adolescence and on to adulthood, from dependency to independence and productivity. Using in-depth interviews with nine different young people and generating a number of interesting "case studies," Randall G. Glading portrays our schools and society at work, giving students in their high school senior year and into college an active chance to participate in "real life" work—interning as scientists, junior firefighters, Broadway theater technicians, gay and lesbian rights advocates, or hospital helpers. Key, it seems, to these adult-building experiences are their reality, activeness, and engagement—unlike instruction in most traditional classrooms that involves passive listening, memorization, and endless testing.

Glading begins with the process, the move from being a teenager to becoming a grown-up, as children are in school longer, starting with preschool and running through high school, and for many going into college that follows. Yet, for all the time and money expended, we have paid little attention to the critical "last step" in the educational process: moving from one A to the next A, from *adolescence* to *adulthood*—from school to work and to participation in family life and society.

What are the active roles of high school and the important senior year in preparing students for adulthood by offering them chances to work as interns, learning from adult mentors in a range of jobs? How might a scientific-minded child, for example, learn adult analytical behavior and insights in a medical or pharmaceutical laboratory? How could a high school senior who is more active be a junior intern for the county fire department and learn to fight fires and help rescue victims—both examples of how schools can help students to model actions and responsibilities as in adulthood?

And this A-to-A continuum, so vital to reaching maturity and making a place in society, is recognized and explained in this informative book by Randall Glading, *Overcoming the Senior Slump*. He puts the high school senior year at the center of the transition

FOREWORD

and determines what these schools can do consciously and actively to help adolescents prepare to be adults. This book starts with interesting cases of real children and how they were helped to grow into adulthood by their schools' running community-based internships, service programs, and other adult-like activities. The book takes us through a five-step journey.

STEP ONE: DEFINING THE TERMINOLOGY

These terms, Adolescence and Adulthood, are hard to define: We know that adolescence, or the so-called teen years, starts when children reach puberty or just before, between ages eleven and fourteen—and then continues to somewhere around twenty-one, when these young adults are able to buy a beer legally, sign contracts, and take their place as grown-ups in society. But kids, at least the girls, are reaching sexual maturity earlier and earlier, and some are even getting pregnant by the time they are twelve or thirteen. Boys, poor things, are lagging behind the girls physically and are taking longer in many cases to reach physical maturity. When I went to my eleven-year-old twin grandchildren's elementary school graduation, the girls in the lines were heads taller than the boys and were showing signs of bosoms while the boys looked like little kids . . . the term "squirt" comes to mind.

Some blame exposure to hormones in food; others say that girls are bombarded with sexual images and stories, perhaps stimulating them physically to mature much faster. So, the start-up of adolescence, physically and socially, is coming earlier and earlier. And the ending of adolescence—and the onset of adulthood—is also being delayed much longer, as students are expected to finish high school by age eighteen or nineteen, attend college for four or five years until, say, about age twenty-two or twenty-three, and then to learn a profession or trade—in graduate school such as law, medical, business, education, or military schools—delaying independent adulthood well into the middle to late twenties.

Adulthood is even more difficult to define: it is in part economic, as adults are expected to be financially independent, equipped to earn a living and support themselves. Social responsibilities are also involved as adults often have family requirements and seek to contribute to their communities and societies. Exactly when adulthood begins is hard to define: for example, does it start when one is inducted into the military (for nations such as Switzerland and Israel require universal military service of all eighteen-year-olds), or when one is accepted into a job and career, opens a bank account, gets married, has children, or buys that first home?

Whatever the exact definitions of adolescence and adulthood may be, formal schooling is starting earlier (kindergarten and now prekindergarten around age four), and it's running longer and longer through adolescence and into the early adulthood years. And the need to introduce adult experiences earlier and more regularly becomes more important—as Glading so well explains in his book.

STEP TWO: CHANGES IN GROWTH

Then the book illustrates powerfully how growing up has changed and the need for schools (high schools and even colleges) to pay closer attention not only to the academic growth and test results (increasing exponentially under the No Child Left Behind law), but also to the social and economic development of students (where they learn skills that will prepare them for jobs and careers). Second, the book ties the stages of development together, from childhood to adolescence to adulthood, a process that is only now being studied, from prekindergarten through high school and college to work and family life.

STEP THREE: CHANGING THE HIGH SCHOOL SENIOR YEAR TO HELP PRODUCE ADULTS

The book makes specific and useful suggestions about how every American high school can begin organizing a range of occupational, social, and community service projects that tie into the high school's curriculum, classroom activities, and programs; how to place students in real-life internships; how best to supervise and mentor students and help them to grow; and thus how to retrieve and bolster the senior year.

As the book explains, internships that include strong mentorships encourage students to gain *independence* as confident, growing, maturing young people; it gives them a real sense of *accomplishment* in what they can do and feel; it helps them to improve their *achievement* in school, college, and beyond, applying what they learned in the field and in the real world.

These experiences help students to create a sense of *passion* about their work and careers, the kind of feelings that some students have held in high school and college athletics and other prominent extracurricular activities (debate, diving, swimming, stamp clubs, spelling bees). Star high school and college athletes and campus leaders enjoy their status and build skill sets of leadership, outstanding personality, and confidence that carry over into adulthood. But not every student has such opportunities to be a Big Man/Woman on Campus (BM[W]OC)—hence the importance of expanding internships for all interested students in both high school and college.

Finally, working in the field gives students a sense of *uniqueness* about themselves—a special skill, gift, talent, drive, and accomplishment—that marks them for adulthood and success in society. Congress and the president are signing a new law, American Competes Act, which is a perfect match for some key internship areas that students can perform; and the law focuses around improving our children's S.T.E.M., an acronym for Science, Technology, Engineering, and Math. This federal program (about to be signed into law) provides areas of learning and practice for high school and college students, where an internship would make S.T.E.M. areas and others come to life.

STEP FOUR: BRINGING COLLEGES INTO THE PROCESS

Glading next takes a good hard look beyond the senior year, at those post–high school experiences too, and how internships (for example, schoolteachers-in-training have long done their "student" or "practice teaching" during their university experience) can help students prepare for the transition to life and work from their university programs. Key to all these field experiences is the mentorship, the adolescent-adult relationships that start formally in high schools, as Glading explains, and continue importantly through college and extend into the job world.

STEP FIVE: PRACTICAL IMPLICATIONS AND ACTIONS

This book is critical for all adults in our society who have responsibility for children—throughout their young lives. High school leaders and teachers need to link learning with performing, giving students a chance to participate in "experiential learning" in every subject area. Growing up means taking responsibility for one's actions and doing something useful and practical that one can be proud of. And as one young person explained, experiential learning helped her to gain the power to make her own decisions.

So, the evidence in this book is clear. Schools should work with the community, giving students a chance to intern—particularly during the important, often wasted senior year—and to get mentoring in real-life jobs in business, science, service associations, and fire and rescue departments. Perhaps a hundred years ago, children grew up faster, learning to farm, milk cows, feed chickens, plow fields, drive tractors, and harvest crops. I remember when teaching junior high school, one of my students was a fourteen-year-old farm boy. He rose at 5:00 a.m. daily and took care of the crops and livestock before coming to school. His parents went on vacation and left him to run the farm.

Most children in modern societies have few chances to run anything or to do jobs that matter. It is thus the responsibility of our parents and teachers to offer teenagers a chance to make a difference, to work in hospitals and shelters, to put out fires, and to help the elderly. Religious associations, scout troops, and service clubs have the right idea. Now it's up to high schools and colleges to build service and practices into the curriculum. Let's imagine the new school, using Glading's approach.

First, students would write an essay on their interests, skills, and concerns. These essays would be reviewed by the high school and college counselors who would establish internships appropriate for the student, based on their interests and skills. Second, students would attend an orientation, run jointly by the school and the internship agency, to explain what the students should do and learn.

Third, after the orientation, the students would meet and work with a group of fellow interns, who have more experience and background. These programs could be for high school or college credit, as a student teacher gets points for practice teaching and interning in the school. Skills learned in a practicum can often be used throughout life, such as learning to make a good public presentation using technology. Take this example of Debbie, one of Glading's good case examples:

> Actually, I remember the first time I presented PowerPoint. It was at JSHS [Junior Science and Humanities Symposium] and I wanted to die. I stuttered and I had no confidence, I was unsure and repetitive,

oh, I read off my notes and it was a miserable experience, absolutely miserable. That was one experience that I kind of drilled in the back of my head that I never want to have happen again.

So, I had to present again later on in tri-county, where I moved on as a semi-finalist. My presentation went so smoothly I didn't know it was me presenting. As for ISEF [Intel Science Talent Search], I never really had a problem presenting one on one, or one, two or three people, because I never had that pressure. I felt like a conversationalist, and as a conversationalist I excelled. I think that was my favorite part of ISEF, I liked convincing people; I was able to sell my project, which is probably the most important aspect of life and science research.

Students can also learn real skills and concepts working in hospitals, fire departments, science centers, social agencies, and media and entertainment. This learning can and does feed back into the academics of schooling and helps students to achieve. It might be a great idea for teachers in social studies, science, and languages, for example, to assign work in the field for students as part of their high school and college work.

Why not interview a survivor of a Nazi concentration camp about World War II? Why not help parents to teach their children English, while learning the primary first language? Why not study the treatment of the common cold or do some AIDS research, using different scientific methods and medicines, and report back to the medical center, tying it to high school or college biological science? And with the rising importance of modern technology, students are at the right age and stage to use the latest computers and software to help with their education and their future as adults.

Parents should be involved, helping their children to find a field or area that interests them; to be placed in an interesting, challenging internship where they can grow; and to get their children the recognition they deserve. Watch the expressions on the faces of parents as their son or daughter hits a home run in a baseball game, wins a debate trophy, or earns standing as an Eagle Scout.

The Glading book makes a strong case for every child's getting these chances under the supportive, proud eyes of their family and friends.

CONCLUSION

Learning about life, building a work ethic, and applying what is being learned to what is going on in the real world—these are the vital lessons taught in the Glading book. And everyone shares a role. Students have primary responsibility for their own lives and growth. Parents want to help their children mature and achieve. Teachers can see chances to get their students into the real world and organize the feedback into their classroom learning and achievement. Schools can reclaim the senior year, and students can gain from attending school and working in the community. And adult job mentors can be recruited and prepared to be key in helping the students to participate and learn in their placements.

Internships will become a key feature of the high school of the future. And the senior year will be a memorable, not a sleepy, wasted year. What are the best places to intern: the fire department, rescue squad, housing services, hospitals, or preschools? Future employers will learn to ask: what kinds of experiences did you have in school and college, and beyond, that will help you be a high performer on your job?

When full preparation for an independent, productive adulthood gets rolling—with job, profession, home, family, children, and community—everyone benefits. This book fills a critical role in the process: helping us to learn just how adolescents grow into productive adults. We know that high schools need to get organized, as do colleges, to have an internship office and trained professionals with close ties to the community to help students to select a set of intern experiences. And students need mentors, skilled job models, whether as a fireman or doctor, social worker, or artist.

Teachers and parents should also be involved to help students to link their schoolwork with their internships and academic learning with their applied learning using rigorous methods—all paving the way for adulthood. What begins in high school continues through college, involving close cooperation among family, school, college, and the working world—all moving students from adolescence to a successful adulthood. Randall Glading's new book breaks new ground, showing us how to relate school, the senior year, and overall education to life in powerful, meaningful ways.

Bruce S. Cooper
Fordham University

ACKNOWLEDGMENTS

First and foremost, I would like to thank the young adults who provided invaluable insight into their internship experience while in high school. Their personal reflections highlight the importance of real-life experiences in high school: providing them with a strong foundation to meet the challenges of postsecondary education.

Special thanks to my sister, JoAstrid Glading, who as editor made these real stories come to life and depict the life of a high school student. Her literary genius provides all of us with clear, concise direction for effective change in public education.

Last but not least, I need to thank Dr. Bruce S. Cooper for his ongoing support. His contribution, the foreword, provides the reader with a comprehensive introduction to the text: taking a critical look at the senior year of high school that reveals several shortcomings of public education.

1

ADOLESCENCE TO ADULTHOOD

Growing up is rarely easy—and making the transition from adolescence to adulthood can be particularly difficult. Young people need help, but most high schools do little to prepare teens for life in college and living an independent adult life.

This book looks at real-life learning experiences, which are often called internships or mentoring programs. These opportunities bridge the gap between adolescence and adulthood and give the adolescent an opportunity to practice adult behaviors. When high schools create internships, they create opportunity for students to benefit from a range of vital experiences that smooth the transition from school to college to work, from dependence to independence, and from an in-between state to one of greater responsibility.

Across the nation, progressive educators are recognizing that internship and mentoring programs can have a profound and positive impact on the high school and college experience. The transition from adolescent to responsible adult can be awkward and difficult. Internship and mentoring programs facilitate this passage while the teenager is still living at home and the structures and supports of family life are still in place. They are given an early—and in most cases a first—opportunity to connect their book and classroom learning with the real world. Much of what they have been taught at home and at school suddenly becomes relevant and the disconnect between the teenager and the adult world begins to dissipate. The "hands-on" experience provides the opportunity for students to become more responsible, confident, and independent—traits that will vastly increase their chances of being successful in college and beyond.

The majority of high school students today will enroll in postsecondary education after graduating high school. And while the number of students who go on to college has steadily risen in the past fifty years, their success rate in college has remained largely unchanged. One recent study found that only 65 percent of the students who enrolled in a four-year college obtained a degree by the time they turned twenty-nine.

Should we be concerned that the public high schools our children attend look much the same as the public schools their parents and grandparents attended? Parents and educators must ask some hard questions about why, after over twenty years of educational reform, we are not doing a better job preparing our children to enter adulthood and succeed in college. We must ask why one-third of all college-bound high school seniors are still failing to even finish college. We must ask ourselves what we can do—and what we must demand our public schools do—to better prepare our sons and daughters to succeed in the adult world that lies outside the walls of their high school. Exposure to the "real world" through experiential learning programs, such as internships and mentoring opportunities, supports the transition from high school to college.

Research has found that the traditional high school experience fosters and maintains a powerful and insular adolescent culture. Parents do not need educational researchers and sociologists to tell them that while our schools move students through the structured and uniform exercise of a public education, teenagers are hard at work building a subculture with their peers that dominates their attentions and energies.

Parents also do not need scholars to tell them that many high school seniors have too much time on their hands, having completed virtually all of their required courses and waiting to hear which colleges will accept them. After an eleven-year marathon of highly structured schooling, and as these students stand on the threshold of adulthood, the demands and expectations we place on them in their senior year suddenly dissipate. Highly motivated students may continue to drive themselves through advanced courses, school activities, or outside employment during their senior year. But for others, after a lifetime of facing rising expectations, suddenly very little is expected of them academically until they go off to college. For many high school seniors, at a time when they should be striving to hone their skills and prepare for more difficult challenges ahead, much of the structure that surrounded them throughout their school experience disappears. Although they may still lack the maturity and judgment to use their newfound freedom wisely, our formal education system gives them little guidance and support during this period.

These are very real facts of life in public high schools: there is a powerful adolescent society that is largely separate from the adult world, and the senior year of high school is underutilized. In that critical senior year we should be preparing teenagers to make the most drastic transition they will ever make, from childhood to the independence of adulthood. Yet our schools are largely failing to meet this challenge.

High schools must recognize the benefits of breaking away from the traditional senior year experience. These students, who stand on the threshold of the real-world, will only benefit if our schools encourage them to engage in real-life internship experiences. This book takes an in-depth look at the high school internship experience of several students, all of whom participated in structured internship programs as an integral part of their secondary education.

We can better understand the significant benefits of participating in an internship program when we view the experience through the eyes of these students, who provide authentic and insightful reflections about their experiences. The following personal reflections of three of the students are examples of defining moments that all of the students experienced and carried with them into adulthood. In each case, the internship experience provided the students with a portal to success and personal growth.

DEBBIE'S STORY

I recall feeling excited and well prepared for my first major science competition. I had worked very hard and practiced my PowerPoint presentation over and over again. But my confidence began to collapse as I watched the contestant before me articulately present his incredibly extensive project on stem-cell research. I was weak and confused during my own presentation, but the experience made me realize that there was more to being a successful presenter than just book research and a fancy PowerPoint program. That incident is now one year behind me. After a year of extensive research, while doing an internship with a well-known pharmaceutical company, my knowledge and confidence soared. I reentered the science competition at the top of my game, the words flowed smoothly, and I was able to make effective and timely eye contact with my audience. I did it; I presented a stunning report on HIV research and advanced to the national competition.

This quiet, introverted adolescent confronted a potentially overwhelming challenge through her experience in a high school internship program. Through this experience, she found her hidden strength and began building a foundation for success in college and beyond. Debbie is currently a premed student at a prestigious university.

PETER'S EXPERIENCE

I still clearly remember the "call" in the middle of a sweltering summer night a few years back. I was clinging to the side of the fire truck as it rolled along the country roads. I could smell the house fire as we approached. Having been with the company for several years, I was no longer frightened and had become much more confident. My colleagues and I went into the structure without hesitation. The rules and guidelines taught in our training had become second nature. We carried the hose through an interior door toward the fire. Suddenly, I felt the floor collapse under me. I struggled to grab something to save me as I yelled to another junior firefighter just a few feet away. Somehow we were able to simultaneously grasp each other's arms, and I was pulled to safety.

I felt a tremendous sense of pride and worth returning to the firehouse that evening, not just because we were successful in salvaging someone's home and precious possessions, but proud to be a part of this great squad. I realized the meaning of brotherhood, the fraternity of firefighters, the unspoken camaraderie. I would give my life for these guys.

Two years later, Peter was a successful sophomore at a prestigious liberal arts college and was still serving as a volunteer firefighter when home from college.

JAMES SPEAKS OUT

As I entered the school cafeteria as a guest speaker to advocate for gay rights, I felt a decidedly chilly response—not from the students, but from the teachers and administrators. Although I felt unwelcome, my courage and confidence prevailed. I was accustomed to not feeling welcome. In fact, up until my senior year of high school I let the perceived prejudices against me all but define me. It was not until I interned at a county agency that advocated gay and lesbian rights that I really began to like and respect myself. Astonishingly, I began to notice that others liked and respected me as well. I became very proud of who I am: determined to let others know that they can feel that way too. My dream is to make the world a better place for gay and lesbian students.

The words I spoke that evening in the school cafeteria were powerful, caring, and straight from my heart. There was a round of applause from the audience at the end of my speech, and as always, I made eye contact with several of the students and knew I made a difference.

James is a graduate of a prestigious university and is pursuing a career in the entertainment field.

These are powerful stories from individuals who participated in high school internships during their senior year of high school. While these students were being shaped by intensive learning experiences, most of their classmates remained behind in a very insulated adolescent world. While these students were learning to find their way in the adult world, most of their peers remained engaged in typical adolescent activities at their respective high schools, many of them already accepted to college and giving little thought to life beyond high school or college.

The individuals you will hear from in this book participated in internship programs that proved to be instrumental in shaping their future and contributing to their success after high school.

Teachers, parents, and students recognize that in many cases, the senior year of high school does not place high academic demands, expectations, or responsibilities on graduating seniors. In sharp contrast, most incoming college students find the freshman year to be academically challenging. But rather than challenging students to prepare for the transition to college, high schools typically allow these young adults to take a step back from academic rigor and commitment during the final months before graduation. In doing so, they allow them to more fully retreat into what researchers have called the "adolescent society." Many professionals believe that this hiatus from academic rigor, high expectations, and responsibility contributes to a student's inability to succeed in college. The lack of academic rigor, combined with the consuming nature of the adolescent culture, conspire to leave these young men and women ill-prepared for the real world and the challenges that lie ahead after graduation.

HIGH SCHOOL AND BEYOND

Each spring American high school communities come together to celebrate the graduation of the senior class, a rite of passage that some view as the ascent of individuals from youth to adulthood. For parents and their children, it is a moment filled with hope and expectation and plans for college.

But with this passage to adulthood, the uncertainty of life begins for many of these young adults. One out of three students headed for college will not graduate. For some of these students, college will be their first encounter with academic failure.

Educators understand the developmental level of children and provide them with age-appropriate educational activities throughout most of high school. School districts spend countless hours reviewing and revising programs, developing curriculum, improving instructional strategies, and providing their teachers with meaningful staff development. Effective pedagogy is the primary focus of our schools, and in a variety of disciplines we use standard exams to measure whether students have learned. Students in public high schools receive an array of services intended to prepare them for life after high school.

At this juncture in the student's life, however, the student may be unclear about future goals and career plans. These graduates have every good intention to succeed in college. Their guidance counselors and schools have worked hard to ensure they have plans for their immediate future according to their individual abilities and interests. High school administrators point to the percentage of students going on to college as a measure of their success in educating students. Yet despite all of the preparation in secondary school and the careful screening of students through the college admissions process, college dropout rates have not changed since the 1950s and 1960s.

Critics have noted that while American education places great importance on the length of time a student remains in school and on obtaining the high school diploma, much less attention is paid to what students need to know to succeed in college. One scholar observed that most young people are "not yet sure where their interests or talents lie; they need to connect with people, ideas, and events to help guide them in their search. Instead, they attend schools that are dissociated from the productive life of the community."[1]

As adults responsible for helping young adults navigate the transition between high school and life after high school, we must do a better job preparing them. We must think outside the box and help them to both disengage from their adolescent society and begin to engage in the broader world that lies beyond high school.

WHAT TO EXPECT

This book examines the short- and long-term effects of high school internship and mentoring programs and whether these programs help young adults prepare for the challenging transition to college and adulthood.

Several students share their stories with us. All of them made a successful transition to college, and several are now in graduate school or the workplace. Their stories and personal reflections provide parents and educators alike with an understanding of the importance of the internship experience. Each individual confronted challenges when they left the safety of their traditional high school programs, and through those experiences they each found opportunities to weave their own tapestry of success. As you read their individual biographies in chapter 5, you will see your child, your nephew, or the child of a good friend. Their stories allow us to look beyond the traditional boundaries of secondary education and explore new instructional initiatives that provide a meaningful connection between what is learned in the classroom and real-life experiences. We also learn through their accounts that their early ventures into the adult world provided powerful experiences that helped them grow and develop critical qualities that would strengthen their foundation for success after high school.

The high school internship experiences provided each of these individuals with the following essential attributes they will need to succeed in adulthood:

Independence
A Sense of Accomplishment
Passion for Learning
Unique Experiences and Challenges in the World of Work
Enhanced Work Ethic
Experience in Building Relationships with Adults

The lesson from their stories is a simple one—educators must confront the shortcomings of public education and change the status quo, which has been accepted for too many decades. Initiatives to provide all high school students with internship opportunities in high school will help to shape the student's secondary experience into a more meaningful preparation for life beyond high school and provide students with a portal to college success and personal growth.

NOTE

1. A. Steinberg, *Real Learning, Real Work* (New York: Routledge, 1998), 5.

2

SECONDARY EDUCATION TODAY

The academic and extracurricular programs of high school are familiar territory for most parents. In this chapter, we will briefly discuss these traditional programs and then take a critical look at the static state of high school education and the sociological pressures and expectations that help shape our public schools. We also will consider the series of reform movements during the past fifty years that sought to change and improve how we educate our children and the principles that underlie a successful learning environment. No analysis of the development of public education would be complete without examining the formidable and insular adolescent society that dominates the typical high school and the impact that phenomenon has on learning. We also will discuss the sociology of this student subculture and its resistance to change.

Finally, we will consider a framework for reform that honors the need for academic rigor but also recognizes that students must develop critical thinking skills and the ability to make their book learning relevant by applying their knowledge to real-life situations. In the course of this journey, they must also learn the skills they will need to take their place in the adult world and begin to build mature adult relationships with those they will soon be working alongside.

The sociology of the adolescent culture that forms within our schools, and the damaging impact it has on the individual growth of students, have been well researched and documented.[1] Our community of educators must take responsibility to look toward innovative programs to counter the negative effects of this adolescent society and create the opportunities students need to mature to adulthood and make the transition to the adult world, especially during the senior year of high school.

ACADEMIC PREPARATION

The primary goal of public education is to prepare our children for future challenges. Secondary education focuses on providing students with a productive high school experience. Schools measure whether or not students are learning through standardized testing.[2] For example, in order to graduate from a public high school in New York State, each student must complete twenty-one credits in their courses of study and successfully pass five Regents examinations, which are traditionally completed prior to the student's senior year of high school. The current standards movement, with its heavy reliance on standardized testing, has its roots in the landmark study more than twenty years ago, *A Nation at Risk*. This focus on measurable academic achievement is echoed in the recent No Child Left Behind legislation.[3]

Teachers realize that society and academic communities focus on student achievement, and the success of their students will be measured by their scores on standardized tests. Throughout high school, students are exposed to various testing situations and are taught strategies to improve their test performance. Their performance in school is rewarded with grades, and college-bound students know their grade point average will be one of the criteria for acceptance into college.[4]

In addition to grade point averages, colleges are provided with another indicator of academic potential. In the junior and senior years of high school, students across America are compared with one another through standardized college admissions tests developed by the College Board. The SAT/ACT examinations are used by universities to determine a student's academic strength, and the tests provide a common benchmark to clarify differences in the academic performance of high school students, regardless of regional variations.[5]

Once the student has established an academic profile by the middle of their junior year, guidance departments work with students to help them navigate the college selection process. Counsel by guidance experts is a vital component to college success, and research indicates that a proper student-institution match is vital to success in college. Parents and their children engage in the college selection process with the expectation that it will result in each student selecting the college or university that is right for them.

EXTRACURRICULAR PROGRAMS

In addition to preparing students academically for the challenges of life, including college, educators also focus on the life of the child in high school. With the recognition that adolescence is a fragile period in an individual's growth, public schools offer a variety of extracurricular activities that are designed to foster the child's interest in certain activities. These activities include athletics, musical ensembles, school publications, community service initiatives, peer tutoring, school governance, communications, and clubs. In many ways, these activities parallel institutions in our society and emulate the greater society within our schools. For example, student governance has always existed in our schools. The electing of class officers emulates the structure of our political system and supports the underlying tenets of our democracy. Individuals who assume leadership roles benefit greatly from the experience and are able to enhance their self-confidence, communication skills, decision-making skills, and ability to work with both peers and adults.

Secondary institutions with a positive school culture offer and promote countless opportunities of this nature. These activities supplement classroom instruction and allow students to grow academically, socially, and emotionally in various venues. Students learn the importance of individual responsibility and active participation in their school, and they assume a role within their high school community. Teachers and parents encourage students to become involved in extracurricular activities and urge them to seek out their niche within the high school and benefit from the experiences that are available. Students can develop their individual talents and interests through their involvement in these programs. This provides the student with a life outside of the academic classroom but still within the confines of the formal school structure. Extracurricular activities can make valuable contributions to the individual growth of students.

Yet despite the range of opportunities offered by our public schools, students do not appear to be any better prepared for succeeding in college now than they were fifty years ago. The college dropout rate has remained largely unchanged. For too many graduating seniors, their high school experiences did not adequately prepare them for the challenges of higher education. This is not a new phenomenon. The educational philosopher John Dewey was an icon of public education. Words he wrote nearly fifty years ago are just as relevant today:

> It is certainly not the fault of teachers that so many of the recent graduates of the school now find themselves at a tragic standstill, without an occupation and without prospect of one. It is not the fault of the

teachers that so many young men and women still in high schools and colleges find themselves in a state of painful and bewildering insecurity about the future. But it is the fault of the system that so many of these young persons have no intellectual legs of their own to stand upon, no sense of perspective by which to take their bearings, no insight into the causes of the economic and social breakdown, and no way of orienting themselves. It is bad enough to be without a job. The evil is increased when these young people find themselves with no clue to the situation in which they are to live and are at a loss intellectually and morally, as well as vocationally and industrially.[6]

The phenomenon Dewey described remains a very real and current problem that demands solutions. When he examined the shortcomings of public education nearly fifty years ago, he pointed to the need to critically look at the high school experience and provide students with the necessary foundation to make a successful transition to their postsecondary pursuits. To solve the problem, we must first acknowledge it.

THE STATIC STATE OF THE INSTITUTION

To face the changing demands of our society, schools must be dynamic social systems that allow students every opportunity to be successful. Our society has placed a premium on a college education, and the attainment of an advanced degree is virtually an expectation for many young adults. The college success rate, however, has changed little in the past forty years.[7] This is compelling evidence that we must identify, revise, and implement strategies that will prepare more students to succeed when they face the difficult transition from high school to college.

There is disagreement as to whether our public schools are properly preparing students for the challenges of higher education. Critics cite the failure of public school systems to meet the societal expectations while defenders of public education point to the fact that more children are attending college than ever before.[8] The argument is again being revisited with the overarching agenda set forth in the No Child Left Behind reform and the ongoing debate surrounding that law. Yet at the secondary level, educational reform movements have failed to increase the percentage of college-bound students who successfully complete their postsecondary course of study.

To understand the new directions in which we need to take our schools, it is helpful to look at where we have been. Most previous education reforms have been the result of clashing social systems and political agendas. Educational reform is a response to formal and informal pressures on public schools, including the cultural expectations of our society.[9] Public schools also have been repeatedly subject to close scrutiny and political pressure as a result of specific events in our society. The industrialization of our country in the early 1900s, the launching of Sputnik in the 1950s, and fears during the Cold War era each generated public concern regarding the adequacy of our education system. One landmark publication, *A Nation at Risk*, also precipitated a close examination of the effectiveness of our public schools.[10]

In a nation with so many opposing views about what underlying tenets should guide our education system, it has proven to be difficult to establish a direction for change that will be both successful and embraced by all constituencies of our society.

Educational reform during the past thirty-five years has centered on several initiatives, including those that focused on the organizational structure of our schools, the philosophy of education, and the revision of curriculum and student assessment. Much research has been done in these areas, and understanding the broad contours of how our public school system came to be is instructive and helpful.

In the early twentieth century, the organizational structure of public education evolved into large bureaucratic systems. The educational philosophy that permeated our academic institutions during the early 1900s mirrored the ethos and values of our developing industrialized nation.[11] The nation needed schools to provide education and training for an industrialized nation, and within this framework a bureaucracy was found to be the most efficient and effective way to exercise authority over the learning and training of young people.[12] These academic institutions sifted individuals and placed them in society according to their talents and their ability to perform social and economic functions. This basic structure of our school systems has remained largely unchanged during the past century but has been repeatedly scrutinized by researchers and education leaders.[13]

In many ways, our public schools are meeting the expectations that society places on them. In the early 1970s, scholar Philip Cusick conducted a study of the "socio-cultural characteristics" of public schools.[14] In his work, *The Student's World,* he reported that these sociocultural features include: "(a) subject area specialization, (b) vertical organization, (c) doctrine of adolescent inferiority, (d) downward communication flow, (e) batch processing of students, (f) routinization of activity, (g) dependence on rules and regulations, (h) future reward orientation, and (i) a supporting physical structure."[15] Of one school that he studied closely, he said: "Horatio Gates High School did what it was supposed to do. That it contained a number of factory-type and bureaucratic type characteristics, even including its shopping-center architecture, is no sheer accident. It emulated the society for which it prepared its students."[16]

The sociocultural aspect of schooling, as described by Cusick, has changed little over the past thirty-five years. Notably, the percentage of high school students who make a successful transition to the postsecondary level has not changed since the Cusick study. Therefore, if we do not question some of the assumptions that underlie the sociocultural characteristics of the public school environment, it is unlikely we will make progress in better preparing students for the challenges that lie beyond high school.

THE ADOLESCENT SOCIETY AND THE STUDENT CULTURE

Through the formation of our public education systems an interesting sociological phenomenon emerged. Philip Cusick called it the "student's world."[17] In his 1961 work, the scholar James Coleman called it the "adolescent society."[18]

It is helpful to view high school in sociological terms as a "maintenance subsystem" of the larger society. Cusick explained in his research that such subsystems serve a number of essential functions:

> The primary duties of the maintenance subsystem of any organization are to (1) socialize new members, (2) teach and enforce society's reward structure, (3) give the society permanence, and (4) insure that the mechanisms designed to implement the productive structure of society are carried out smoothly and their disruption prevented.[19]

Researchers have observed that while schools are one of the maintenance subsystems of our society, the effectiveness of our schools is challenged by certain realities of the adolescent society.[20] The morals and ethos of the students' world are far more powerful than the external societal and parental expectation that students must perform well in school. While the formation of the adolescent society may be an unintended consequence of how we have structured public schools, the result is a highly insular society that allows students to further organize themselves into smaller student groups or cliques. Research indicates that the educational goals of this maintenance subsystem, or high school, are not embraced by the students themselves. Rather, in his 1973 research, Cusick found that students "have responded by paying only a minimal amount of forced attention to 'formal' educational processes and simultaneously channeled their energy and enthusiasm into their groups wherein lie the more immediate rewards of activity, interest, and involvement."[21]

Another researcher, L. M. Hoffman, identified the same phenomena nearly thirty-five years later when she undertook a study of what high school yearbooks reveal about the high school experience. As with Cusick, she reported that "the students demonstrated a lack of interest in their academic work through their oral and written responses, and . . . stressed the importance of the adolescent ethos and rites of passage in their schools"[22]

There is no question that the adolescent culture has a significant impact on the individual development of students and that schools have largely fostered the development of this adolescent society that is separate and apart from society as a whole. Coleman described the insular nature of this adolescent society in powerful terms:

> The setting apart of our children in schools—which take on ever more functions, ever more "extracurricular activities"—for an ever longer period of training, has a singular impact on the child of high-school age. He is cut off from the rest of society, forced inward toward his own age group, made to carry out his whole social life with others of his own age. With his fellows, he comes to constitute a small society, one that has most of its important interactions within itself, and maintains only a few threads of connection with the outside adult society. In our modern world of mass communication and rapid diffusion of ideas and knowledge, it is hard to realize that separate subcultures can exist right under the very noses of adults—subcultures with languages their own, with entire special symbols, and, most importantly, with value systems that may differ from adults.[23]

Coleman's research came several decades before the proliferation of cell phones and e-mail, and long before the emergence of MySpace, instant messaging, text messaging, and the countless other ways in which members of the adolescent society maintain and build their connections with one another outside the presence of adults. Coleman's research indicates that in the educational setting, the ethos and values of the adolescent culture may differ greatly from the traditional beliefs of the adults who founded our established educational bureaucracies. Furthermore, only a small portion of the school day is actually dedicated to engaging students in teacher directed instruction.

> Schools demand attendance, passive compliance, and limited attention but not a lot more. Adding up the time spent on announcements or receiving assignments, coming and going, eating, waiting, and watching, and otherwise complying with the procedural demands, students experience a great deal of empty space in the day. . . . One student from Cusick's work stated, "You're only with teachers 30 percent of the time in school, the other two-thirds are just talking."[24]

Throughout the school day, students are placed into small formal groups for the purposes of instruction. But for most students these classes, or groups, cannot compete with the draw of the adolescent society:

> The fact is that for many students, adult guided, academic endeavors are not sufficiently attractive to offset the intensity and exhilaration offered by the ever-present groups. The group, or best friend, or simply "friend," is usually present in class and in an idle moment or when the teacher's attention is distracted or an interruption occurs; a glance can bring contact and the whole world of shared perceptions, private jokes, and interests are awakened. Students slide easily from class to group activity.[25]

This being the norm, it raises the question of whether the traditional pedagogy that is ingrained in our public education system, or the system itself, is preparing our students for the challenges of higher education and the real world. What is certain, however, is that the distractions of the adolescent society continually compete with the mission of the classroom.

The adolescent society is an integral part of the high school student culture. Within any society, there are fundamental values and beliefs that guide an individual's behavior and decision making. Philosophers and sociologists have always recognized the importance of moral rules within any society. These rules are established on an individual basis and within society itself. These moral rules exist within any society, independent of the individual. This sense of society has been described as both something beyond us and something in ourselves.[26] While the individuals within the society are perpetually replaced by others, the society's moral foundation will endure over the years. This also is a characteristic of the society that we call school. Within this society there is a student subculture, which both Cusick and Coleman identified in their research. These cultures appear to be enduring and consistent over time, and we must consider this social phenomenon when we study our educational institutions. In some ways, this unified adolescent culture can be compared to some religious groups:

> The stronger the credo of a religious group, the more unified it is likely to be, and therefore better able to provide an environment that will effectively insulate its members from perturbing and frustrating experiences.[27]

Students in public high school have developed extremely powerful and insular cultures. The phenomenon, observed by researchers more than forty years ago, is alive and well in public schools today. In her work, L. M. Hoffman used the school yearbook as an instructive artifact of adolescent culture within high school. Even an informal review of school yearbooks reveals that socially accepted activities and the basic operating structure of public high schools have changed very little over time.

Hoffman examined several aspects of the production of the school yearbook and used focus group interviews and surveys to conduct her research. She also examined the yearbooks themselves to gain more information regarding the elements of adolescent ethos, which included getting along with peers, being involved in activities, gaining independence, and specific rites of passage.[28] Like Cusick and Coleman before her, she concluded that the primary focus of the students was their relationships with their friends and acquaintances, and they demonstrated a lack of interest in their schoolwork.[29]

In many ways, high school students who do not plan to go to college and instead pursue vocational training are foisted into the adult world earlier. Much of their high school learning centers on highly practical knowledge that is clearly relevant and useful to their post–high school plans. Likewise, students who enter trade school from high school are already exercising adult choices about the field in which they wish to work and are encouraged and supported to leave the insulated adolescent world as they prepare to work in a trade.

The work of Hoffman and others clearly supports the need for schools to change. Within the four walls of any high school, there is a student culture that is resistant to learning. The forces of the student culture provide adolescents with comfort and a feeling of success among their close network of peers. There are many rites of passage, ceremonies, and rituals that students experience during the four years of high school:

> From freshman initiation through sophomore, junior, and senior years, each year/class group experienced increasing opportunities for mobility in the student prestige hierarchy, increasing access as a group to the commercial enterprises of the system, increasing financial affluence of the class-group, increasing political power and responsibility for important ceremonial events, and increasing self-regulation of the subsystem.[30]

Surely, when students are incorporated within this adolescent society in high school, it has a dramatic impact on them during these critically formative years. They are not challenged to grow and learn as they would be outside of the comfort zone of their peers. As they near the responsibilities of independence and young adulthood, they are not challenged to meet the more demanding standards of the adult world. But if students are given experiential learning opportunities to move outside of their adolescent world and begin the transition into the adult world, the dynamics of the adolescent society will begin to break down in powerful and positive ways, and we will better prepare our children for life after high school.

THE THREE R'S REVISITED: RIGOR, RELEVANCE, RELATIONSHIPS[31]

Secondary schools have always been accountable for maintaining academic rigor. The recent standards movement once again reinforced that academic rigor must be the focus of all schooling from kindergarten through twelfth grade. At times, however, we question the relevance of certain book knowledge that is mandated in our public schools. As adults, at times we are at a loss when our children ask us, "Why do I need to know this?" There is a disconnect between what we are taught in school and understanding how that knowledge can be applied in the real world.

There is also justifiable concern across the country regarding the standards movement and the new accountability placed on our public schools. The mandates set forth in the No Child Left Behind reform expect schools to improve student achievement, which is certainly a worthy goal. There are many concerns, however, over the effectiveness of evaluating learning through quantitative, standardized tests that require students to recall information. Educators are being held accountable, and their schools are expected to show yearly progress in student achievement through these standardized tests, but at what cost? School districts are scrambling to fund academic intervention services for many students to improve their performance.

We must question, however, whether these are the right strategies and whether they will actually improve learning by students. Thoughtful researchers have long contended that quantitative, standardized tests measure only the student's knowledge of a subject, and this type of knowledge is the lowest form of critical thinking and intellectual behavior.[32] While we may successfully convey information, which students can report back on a test, we are not necessarily teaching children how to think. Regardless of one's viewpoint in the standards debate, it remains clear that schools must do more than just teach students to pass standardized exams. They must teach students to become successful adults who can bring critical thinking skills to the challenges of life.

If we want to maintain true academic rigor in our schools, we must recognize that sufficient questions have been raised about the intellectual engagement of students in their high school academics. We also must be willing to search for solutions to the shortcomings of our schools.

The challenge for public schools is to both provide opportunities for students to engage in activities that elicit higher order thinking skills and then help students understand the relevance of this knowledge by applying their learning to real-life situations. The work of Dr. Willard Daggett provides a framework to evaluate how well we are transferring usable and relevant knowledge to students.

In 1991, Dr. Daggett established the International Center for Leadership in Education. The center developed a framework for academic rigor and relevance that is used by many districts in their charge to improve the academic performance on state examinations and promote educational reform within their district. The academy defines academic excellence as the ability of schools to promote high levels of academic rigor while making the learning relevant to the student's life.[33] The framework is included in figure 1.

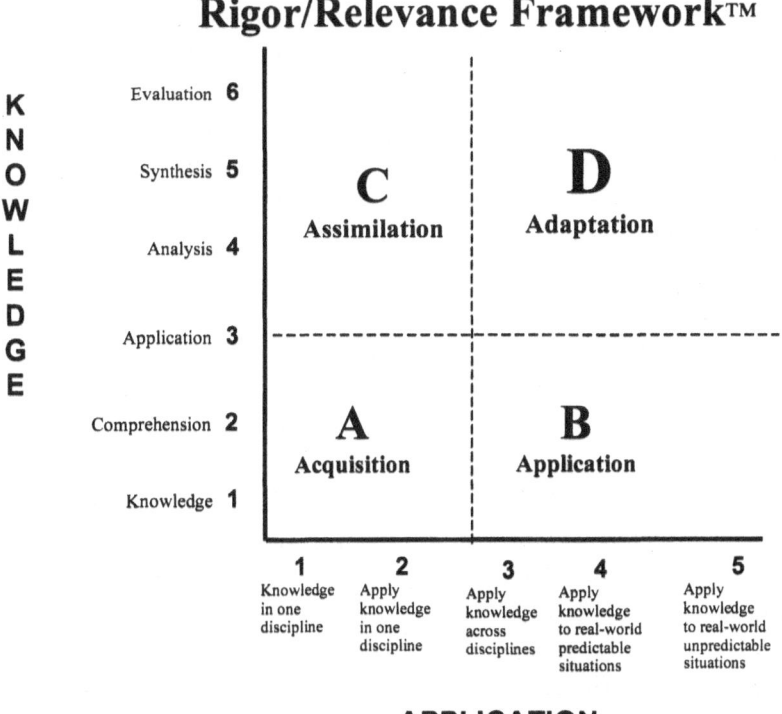

Figure 1. Framework for academic rigor and relevance from the International Center for Leadership in Education. Used with permission of the International Center for Leadership in Education (see www.LeaderEd.com).

The paradigm is quite similar to the continuum of intellectual engagement that was developed by researcher Benjamin Bloom in the 1950s. The finding that we must work to provide higher levels of inquiry and understanding and foster higher level thinking skills is a challenge to the status quo of the standards-based public schooling that we offer many of our students. The Rigor and Relevance paradigm places intellectual behavior along a continuum, and the highest level of that continuum is one's ability to "apply knowledge to real-world unpredictable situations."[3,4]

Dr. Daggett makes a compelling case for why students learn best when they have the opportunity to apply what they have learned in real and relevant settings. A copy of his position paper can be found in Appendix A. Academic rigor and relevance are the foundation of the internship programs that are examined in this book.

But rigor and relevance alone are not enough to ensure students learn the skills they need to become successful college students and adults. They also must learn to form productive, rewarding relationships with adults. It is not uncommon for students to develop appropriate relationships with adults during their tenure in high school. These relationships are critical to the social and emotional development of the adolescent and may be developed with certain teachers, administrators, counselors, advisors, coaches, and support staff.

The reflections of the students presented later in this text demonstrate the essential importance of giving adolescents the opportunity to develop relationships with other adults outside of the traditional boundaries of high school. From the vantage point of these students, it is vividly clear that their internship experiences challenged them to learn how to build meaningful relationships with adults. What they learned through those experiences provided them with a strong foundation to develop mature adult relationships when they left the relative safety of their high school for college.

NOTES

1. J. Coleman, *The Adolescent Society* (New York: Glencoe, 1961); P. Cusick, *Inside High School: The Student's World* (New York: Holt, Reinhart, Winston, 1973); L. M. Hoffman, "Why High Schools Don't Change: What Students and Their Yearbooks Tell Us," *High School Journal* 86, no. 2 (2002): 22–37.

2. E. D. Hirsch, Jr., *The Schools We Need: Why We Don't Have Them* (New York: Doubleday, 1996).

3. R. Paige, *No Child Left Behind: A Parents Guide* (Washington, DC: Education Publications Center, 2003).

4. A. Astin, *What Matters in College? Four Critical Years Revisited* (San Francisco: Jossey-Bass, 1993).

5. M. Kirst and A. Venezia, *From High School to College: Improving Opportunities for Success in Postsecondary Education* (San Francisco: Jossey-Bass, 2004).

6. J. Dewey, *Philosophy of Education* (Totowa, NJ: Littlefield, Adams, 1958), 90.

7. Kirst and Venezia, *From High School to College*.

8. G. Orfield and M. Kornhaber, *Raising Standards or Raising Barriers* (New York: Century Foundation, 2001).

9. R. Callahan, *Education and the Cult of Efficiency* (Chicago: University of Chicago Press, 1962).

10. Hirsch, *The Schools We Need*; Kirst and Venezia, *From High School to College*.

11. Callahan, *Education and the Cult of Efficiency*.

12. M. Weber, *Max Weber on Law in Economy and Society* (New York: Simon and Schuster, 1968).

13. Callahan, *Education and the Cult of Efficiency*; Hirsch, *The Schools We Need*; W. Glasser, *The Quality School: Managing Students without Coercion* (New York: HarperCollins, 1990).

14. Cusick, *Inside High School*, 208.
15. Cusick, *Inside High School*, 208–9.
16. Cusick, *Inside High School*, 221.
17. Cusick, *Inside High School*.
18. Coleman, *The Adolescent Society*.
19. Cusick, *Inside High School*, 220.
20. M. Bradley, *Yes, Your Teen Is Crazy* (Gig Harbor, WA: Harbor, 2002); Cusick, *Inside High School*, 1; Glasser, *The Quality School*.
21. Cusick, *Inside High School*, 222.
22. Hoffman, "Why High Schools Don't Change," 1.
23. Coleman, *The Adolescent Society*, 3.
24. Cusick, *Inside High School*, 32.
25. Cusick, *Inside High School*, 33.
26. A. Bancroft and S. Rogers, "Emile Durkheim—The Work," Introduction to Social Theory: Social Theory On-Line, 2004 (retrieved

January 28, 2004, from www.cf.ac.uk/socsi/undergraduate/introsoc/durkheim.html).
27. Bancroft and Rogers, "Emile Durkheim—The Work," 2.
28. Hoffman, "Why High Schools Don't Change."
29. Bradley, *Yes, Your Teen Is Crazy*; Hoffman, "Why High Schools Don't Change"; N. Noddings, *The Challenge to Care in Schools* (New York: The Teachers College Press, 1992).
30. Hoffman, "Why High Schools Don't Change."
31. Willard R. Daggett's excellent paper, "Achieving Academic Excellence through Rigor and Relevance," September 2005, is included in the appendix. We supplement Dr. Daggett's Rigor and Relevance paradigm with Relationships because they emerged as such an essential part of the mentoring and internship experience. Please see www.LeaderEd.com.
32. B. Bloom, *Taxonomy of Educational Objectives: The Classification of Educational Goals* (New York: David McKay, 1956); Daggett, "Achieving Academic Excellence," 2005.
33. Daggett, "Achieving Academic Excellence," 2005.
34. Daggett, "Achieving Academic Excellence," 2005.

THE POSTSECONDARY EXPERIENCE

There is no question that for most incoming freshmen, the college experience is filled with new challenges, from managing new and unfamiliar independence to handling rigorous academic coursework that is more difficult than anything they encountered in high school. The transition to college also is fraught with the risk of failure. Only 65 percent of incoming freshmen will graduate, a statistic that has remained largely unchanged for more than forty years. This chapter discusses some of the research into the college departure puzzle.

There are no simple answers as to why about one-third of incoming college students drop out without obtaining a degree. It is clear, however, that the reasons include more than just financial problems. Researchers have found that for many students, psychological or emotional issues influenced the decision to leave college.

This chapter also takes a detour into social anthropology, which helps us understand the complex and challenging transition from high school to college. From the standpoint of a social anthropologist, this transition is part of the passage to adulthood and it requires adolescents to separate from their social supports in high school so that they can transition into a new community. We then discuss some of the strategies that colleges have undertaken to help students through this stressful and disorienting transition.

LIFE AFTER HIGH SCHOOL— THE COLLEGE EXPERIENCE

The students who provided their personal reflections for this text represent typical college students and the range of different experiences one can expect in postsecondary education. Several of the students considered themselves to be average students in high school and attended either a small liberal arts college or a school that was part of a state university system. Other students we spoke to were accepted to extremely prestigious universities because they had been high achievers in high school. Many of the students we spoke to went away to college, while others elected to stay home and commute to college due to family obligations and financial constraints.

The interviews revealed that the postsecondary experience was challenging to all of the students in many ways. The students embraced the transition to adulthood but reflected on the various hurdles they felt they needed to clear in order to succeed. Even the valedictorian of a high school faced challenges he had never experienced before when he arrived at college. But he was able to work through the demands of the prestigious university and regain his footing by the second semester of his freshman year. The students also spoke about their efforts to be accepted into the college society and how they emotionally and socially needed to travel down many paths that were unfamiliar to them.

After thirteen years of public education, these students stood on the threshold of their future. They shared with us the challenging nature of this experience. All of the students in this text eventually had a successful college experience. Unfortunately, this is not the norm, and a large percentage of college bound students will not succeed in college. This phenomenon, the college departure puzzle, has existed for more than forty years and continues to plague young adults and postsecondary institutions. Yet while it is stark reality that has remained largely unchanged, it is the eight-hundred-pound gorilla in the room. Parents and high school educators do not readily acknowledge the likelihood of failure in college. For many parents and students, dropping out of college becomes the first experience with academic failure. Yet when we fail to honestly acknowledge the problem, we cannot honestly address the strategies and reforms needed to address the problem.

THE COLLEGE DEPARTURE PUZZLE

The complexion of higher education drastically changed after the Second World War. The expansion in the number and size of our universities, which started in the late 1940s and continued through the 1960s, reflected the response by our federal government to a changing world. More than 1.1 million soldiers embraced the G.I. Bill as an opportunity to enhance their education. A decade later, the government responded to the launching of Sputnik by enacting the National Defense Education Act of 1958, followed by the Higher Education Act of 1965. These events greatly impacted and changed the place of higher education in our society.[1]

Rapid increases in enrollment, along with an increased expectation that more students should go to college, placed additional strain on colleges and university systems. Postsecondary institutions did not, however, forecast the increase in the dropout rate that was to come and the inability of many students to succeed at the postsecondary level. Student retention and the college dropout rate became a major concern.

Extensive research has been done in the area of student retention in college, dating back as early as 1937. Researchers have described the college "departure puzzle" in many different ways:

> The terminology to describe this phenomenon has changed over time and includes descriptors such as student mortality (McNeely 1937; Gekowski & Schwartz 1961), college dropouts (Summerskill 1962; Spady 1971; Tinto 1975), student attrition (Sexton 1965; Panos & Astin 1967; Pantages & Creedon 1978; Tinto 1993), college retention (Iffert 1957; Tinto1990; Berger 2002; Braxton & Mundy 2002), and student persistence (Berger & Milem 1999; Berger 2002).[2]

The college departure problem continues today. In 1993, of the 2.4 million students enrolled in higher education approximately 1.1 million never received a degree.[3] Data as recent as 1998 revealed that only 65 percent of the students who enrolled in a four-year school received a bachelor's degree by the age of twenty-nine.[4]

There has been exhaustive research into the college departure problem. Two experts in the field, Alexander Astin and Vincent Tinto, offer very different but equally helpful perspectives on the underlying components of student retention at the postsecondary level.[5] Astin examined the phenomenon from several viewpoints, including the organization of higher education, family background, and the psychological factors that influence the new college student.[6] Tinto's work is grounded in the field of social anthropology.[7]

Between 1968 and 1972, data was collected on the experiences of more than forty thousand college students as part of a research project conducted by the Cooperative Institutional Research Program (CIRP) in concert with the American Council on Education and the University of California's Laboratory for Research on Higher Education.

The data identified several reasons for dropping out that are self-evident, such as financial problems or poor grades. When

Astin analyzed this massive body of data, however, he concluded that there are a multitude of factors that significantly influence whether or not a student is successful in college. Astin recognized that many intervening variables can impact a student's chance of success in college. In his research, he examined relevant data about the student's family background, academic performance, employment, financial aid, high school experiences, family structure, race, and gender, as well as information about the characteristics of the college the student attended. The reasons cited by Astin in his 1975 analysis raise serious questions.

He found that students left college not only because of financial problems or bad grades. They also dropped out because of psychological or emotional reasons, were bored with their courses, experienced a change in family responsibilities, were dissatisfied with the institutional requirements of college, or changed their career goals.[8]

His work is an important recognition of the fact that there is an underlying psychological component to student persistence in college. This in turn raises the questions of whether students left high school without the proper psychological preparation to succeed in college and what we can do to better prepare them for the demanding transition to college.

In attempting to solve the college departure puzzle, research that is grounded in psychological theories has focused on the educational persistence of the individual student. These researchers have viewed the student's ability to meet the academic demands of college, as well as the individual's personality, motivation, and disposition, as vital predictors of academic success.[9] When Tinto conducted his research in 1993, however, he examined the problem solely from a social anthropological perspective.

Tinto's theory about the reasons for the college departure problem draws heavily on the work of Arnold Van Gennep, a Dutch anthropologist. Van Gennep compared the transition of a young adult to an institute of higher learning with certain rites of passage in a tribal society. His analogy examined "the movement of individuals from membership in one group to that in another, especially as it occurs in the ascent of individuals from youth to adult status in society."[10] This passage to adulthood is just as relevant and real in our modern society. Tinto found that students making the transition from high school to college experienced three distinct phases or stages: "separation, transition and incorporation," and these stages "move individuals from youthful participation to full adult membership in society."[11]

Many new college students are changing membership to a new community. Leaving the comfort of home and the emotional and supportive assurance of their high school friends marks the first stage as described by Tinto. Separation from these groups is essential if the individual is going to be able to become incorporated within the next community. Tinto observed, however, that a student who is "dealing with this separation, combined with one's personality and the character of the institution, may encounter problems of adjustment whose resolution may well spell the difference between continued persistence and early departure."[12] The individual's new community and previous community may differ in values, norms, and behavioral and intellectual styles. Yet in order to become a member of the new community, the individual is required to separate from the former community, which can be stressful, isolating, and disorienting.[13]

The second stage of this passage from one community to another is *transition*. The individual must learn to interact in new ways with the members of the new group, adapt to the new environment, and adopt the socially accepted norms and behaviors that characterize the community. Individuals also must seek out their new role within the group, something they did several years earlier when they began their high school years.

The final stage as described by Van Gennep is *incorporation*, which requires the individual to be accepted as a competent member of the group for full acceptance. This includes participation in special ceremonies that mark full acceptance by the group, allowing the individual to reap rewards from the new community and requiring the individual to assume certain responsibilities as a fully accepted member of the group.[14]

This passage is a complex and challenging one for an individual who is moving from high school to college and from adolescence to adulthood. Not only is the individual often leaving a highly insular adolescent society behind and entering the much more expansive and demanding culture of a college campus, the student also is often leaving home for the first time and making this transition without the daily support of family and friends.

THE POSTSECONDARY PERSPECTIVE—
TRANSITION STRATEGIES

When examining the transition to college, we must scrutinize what high schools do to prepare students. It is just as important, however, to examine what meets the individual on the other side of the bridge when the student arrives at college.

While secondary educators must reflect upon the experiences that they are providing for their students during the four years of high school, postsecondary institutions must understand and identify the hurdles an individual must clear in order to succeed in college.

The leaders of postsecondary institutions are concerned about the inability of incoming students to succeed at the university level. College and university leaders have incorporated freshman seminar programs to support the students in their transition to college. The National Resource Center for the First Year Experience (2000), which is housed at the University of South Carolina, found that 749 colleges and universities offered freshman seminar programs.[15] The mission of the center is to "build and sustain a vibrant campus-based and international educational community committed to the success of first-year college students and all students in transition."[16]

An examination of some of the initiatives that postsecondary institutions have undertaken demonstrates the concern of leaders at the college or university level with the need to enhance the success and retention rate of students at their schools.

For example, Dickinson State University, a small rural liberal arts school in North Dakota, has a freshman class of approximately four hundred students, similar in size to many suburban high schools in New York State. In the 1997–1998 school year, the university was concerned with a freshman retention rate of less than 54 percent. A task force was formed and its first initiative was to formalize the school's freshman seminar program so that it would be taught by faculty with a focus on academics and transitioning to college. The program also was designed to serve as a cornerstone for the establishment of smaller learning communities, providing students with the academic, social, and emotional support they needed. The retention rate for freshman students jumped to 73 percent over the course of three years, and record enrollments were recorded.[17]

At Cortland State University, a small college in upstate New York that is part of the state university system, all freshman students are required to enroll in COR101, The Cortland Experience. The course is "specifically designed to facilitate the intellectual and social integration of all incoming freshman as they make their transition to SUNY Cortland."[18] Requiring this course of all incoming freshman clearly represents an effort to formally counsel students on their transition to university life. The curriculum emphasizes the development of critical thinking skills, the promotion of active reading and writing, the development of personal goals, and the importance of maintaining a balanced and healthy lifestyle, all of which are deemed necessary to success at the postsecondary level.[19]

The University of Maryland, one of the largest universities in that state, offers more than one hundred class sections of UNIV

100 and 101, seminars that are sponsored by the orientation office to support the transition of entering students. The classes are staffed by either a faculty member or a pair of teaching assistants, demonstrating that the university clearly considers the program a vital component of the freshman experience. The class size is limited to twenty-five students, allowing the experience to be more personal and to provide for peer mentoring and support. All students are encouraged to enroll in the program.[20]

At Princeton University in New Jersey, students enroll in the Program of Freshman Seminars in the Residential Colleges. The theme-based, small group structure of these seminars provides each student with the opportunity to establish a relationship with other members in the class and, most importantly, with a faculty member. Engaging conversation continues during informal meetings and provides the students with a mentoring relationship. The Writing Program also is available to freshman students at Princeton. The program emphasizes writing skills and provides students with an in-depth analysis of their writing proficiency. Students are encouraged to enroll in these courses during their first year at Princeton.[21]

Extensive research, recently conducted by Dr. Tom Ellett as part of his doctoral dissertation at Fordham University, examined the implementation of smaller learning communities: theme-based housing and residential colleges similar to the program at Princeton University. He found that "through intentionally 'engineered' structured living units, such as residential colleges, learning communities, and themed floors, students have the opportunity to be in programs that support their personal growth and development in a holistic manner."[22]

These four programs are all efforts by university officials to address the departure puzzle by investing resources in providing transitional help for new students. For most entering freshmen, the university experience presents a drastic lifestyle change. For the first time students must establish independent study habits, manage their time properly, establish a new peer support group, and succeed without the supports they relied upon during their high school years. Ellett found that higher education institutions are fully aware of the challenge of this transition and the need for programs designed to make the transition a successful one:

> A student's involvement begins prior to his or her arrival. The process begins at the time of recruitment. High school on-campus summer programs, admission overnight weekend programs, and invitations to attend summer orientation programs are a few of the techniques institutions are using to welcome students to their new homes. Once students arrive they are greeted with programs to educate them about on-campus resources and suggest strategies for succeeding at their new institution.[23]

Programs like these are an effort by institutions of higher learning to make the transition from high school to college as seamless as possible. At the same time, there is a growing movement in high schools across the country to supplement the academic experience of their students with innovative internship and mentoring opportunities. These programs provide experiential learning opportunities that support independent learning, require students to manage their time, and create the opportunity to become a member of a learning community outside of the traditional classroom. Educational offerings like these are being phased into the mainstream curriculum in many high schools.

NOTES

1. A. Seidman, *College Student Retention* (Westport, CT: Praeger, 2005).
2. Seidman, *College Student Retention*, 7.
3. V. Tinto, *Leaving College: Rethinking the Causes and Cures of Student Attrition* (Chicago: University of Chicago Press, 1993).

4. M. Kirst and A. Venezia, *From High School to College: Improving Opportunities for Success in Postsecondary Education* (San Francisco: Jossey-Bass, 2004).
5. Tinto, *Leaving College*; A. Astin, *Preventing Students from Dropping Out* (San Francisco: Jossey-Bass,1975).
6. Astin, *Preventing Students from Dropping Out*.
7. Tinto, *Leaving College*.
8. Astin, *Preventing Students from Dropping Out*.
9. Tinto, *Leaving College*.
10. Tinto, *Leaving College*, 92.
11. Tinto, *Leaving College*, 92.
12. Tinto, *Leaving College*, 94.
13. Tinto, *Leaving College*.
14. Tinto, *Leaving College*.
15. T. E. Ellett, *Building Engagement in Urban Universities: A Student Perspective on Residential Learning Communities* (PhD diss.) (New York: Fordham University, 2005).
16. University of South Carolina, "National Resource Center for the First-Year Experience," 2005 (retrieved December 10, 2005, from www.sc.edu/fye).
17. University of South Carolina, "International Conference on the First-Year Experience," 2003 (retrieved December 12, 2004, from http://www.sc.edu/fye/events/presentation/international2003/ppt/1).
18. SUNY Cortland, "COR 101: The Cortland Experience," 2004 (retrieved December 12, 2004, from http://www.cortland.edu/advisement/COR101/index.html), 1.
19. SUNY Cortland, "COR 101: The Cortland Experience."
20. University of Maryland Orientation, "Univ Classes: New Student Seminars That Help You Achieve," 2004 (retrieved December 12, 2004, from http://www.orientation.umd.edu/univ/univ_1_welcome.html).
21. Princeton Freshman Seminars, "Introduction to the Program of Freshman Seminars in the Residential Colleges," 2004–2005 (retrieved January, 24, 2005, from http://www.princeton.edu/pr/pub/fs/04/01.html).
22. Ellett, *Building Engagement in Urban Universities*, 9.
23. Ellett, *Building Engagement in Urban Universities*, 5–6.

4

THE INTERNSHIP MOVEMENT

This book is based on an inquiry into successful high school internship programs in several school districts. The directors of these programs provided invaluable insight into the intricacies and challenges of building successful internship programs. In chapters 5, 6, and 7, we will hear the reflections from the students who participated in these programs, their experiences, and their thoughts about how these opportunities prepared them for life beyond high school. This chapter examines several internship programs, the implementation of those programs in public schools, and the philosophical framework that supports experiential learning opportunities as both effective and critical to individual growth.

One example of an overwhelmingly successful internship program is the Big Picture Company. The concept evolved from the conversations of Dennis Littky, Elliot Washor, and Deborah Meier at the Annenburg Institute for Educational Reform at Brown University. It is an example of a nonprofit educational design organization, and it made its initial mark at the Metropolitan Regional Career and Technical Center (the Met) in Providence, Rhode Island. At the Met, founders Littky and Washor have had a profound impact on the lives of students who had a history of poor academic performance and little hope of attending college. Currently, 90 percent of their students apply to college with an acceptance rate of 98 percent.

When the founders of the program asked themselves "what's best for kids, and built everything around the answers," internship and experiential learning opportunities came to the forefront.[1] One of the basic tenets of the internship initiative at the Met is to facilitate authentic learning experiences for students:

> A person's deepest learning usually results from authentic experiences.... such as work with a mentor at a job or community service project, motivate profound learning for several reasons.... The work has real consequences.... The resources for learning are limitless when students are not confined to one building and a predetermined set of materials.... The student develops personal relationships with experts in areas of his passion.[2]

Because of the propensity of public education to resist innovation, the Met faced challenges in its infancy. But the directors believed that the internship program was central to their success and pursued that vision. When Trish McNeil, then deputy secretary for the U.S. Department of Education, examined the program, she said, "I have never seen a school where internships play such an important role in the education of the student as they do here."[3]

The popularity of the internship movement has increased over the past several years due to the popularity of initiatives like the Big Picture Company and the evolution of organizations such as WISE, Science Research programs, and an emphasis on community service. These organizations have provided school districts with options when they consider starting a student internship and mentoring program. The directors and consultants for these programs understand the fixed boundaries of traditional public education and carefully identify where experiential learning programs can fit within school systems across the country. The founders of these programs hold fast to the belief that all students can benefit from the internship experience.

SCIENCE RESEARCH MENTORING PROGRAMS

One of the mentoring programs we studied is the Science Research Program. These programs are offered across the country in public high schools and provide the opportunity for students to participate in science competitions at the local, regional, and national level. For the purpose of this study, we will focus on Science Research programs offered in high schools in Westchester County, New York. Students enroll in the Science Research Program in addition to their required core subjects in the area of science. The students receive credit for the course as elective credit towards their graduation requirement. The students can enroll in the program as early as their sophomore year in high school and can receive up to twelve college-level credits through the State University of New York at Albany.

Under the tutelage of a faculty advisor, the students develop an original research project, and at the same time they seek out a mentor who is a specialist in that particular field of study. Their research is monitored under the supervision of their mentor, with most of their research being conducted during the two summers between their sophomore and senior years of high school. The nature of the research requires their work to be conducted in the laboratory setting provided by or arranged for by their mentor. For example, one student who was conducting a project on stem-cell research was able to find a mentor at a renowned science research facility in New York City.

The students work on their research project independently during an assigned period within the school day. Although the advisor is available for counsel and support, most of the work done during the day is conducted online using professional scientific databases.

The advisor monitors student progress, processes students for the upcoming competitions, and is always reaching out to provide support for students who may be experiencing difficulty. Students spend most of their time working independently on their projects after school, during evenings, and on weekends. Regular meetings are scheduled with their mentor during the school year and also during the summers.

The students enter competitions at the local, regional, and national levels at different times during the school year. The students are expected to present their research project using a prescribed format, and the judges are experts in various fields of science. The renowned competitions that the students enter are the Westchester Science and Engineering Fair, the Intel Science Talent Search, the Siemans/Westinghouse Science Competition, the Junior Science & Humanities Symposium, the Tri-County Science Fair, and the Intel International Science and Engineering Fair.

The students involved in science research programs of this nature are required to work independently, engage in a high level of academic rigor and research, work outside of their traditional high school setting, and develop relationships with adults who are experts in their field of study. Motivation, enthusiasm, and dedication are the essential prerequisites to success in these programs.

These same qualities are required in the WISE Program, another school-based mentoring/internship program offered to high school seniors.

WISE INTERNSHIP PROGRAM

The WISE Program was founded by Vic Leviatin at Woodlands High School in Hartsdale, New York, during the 1972–1973 school year. The acronym WISE originally stood for the Woodlands Individualized Senior Experience. With the gain in popularity of the program, many schools seek out assistance from Mr. Leviatin and his program, now called WISE Services. Mr. Leviatin, now a retired teacher, travels to school districts throughout the country to provide educational leaders, teachers, and students with assistance in the establishment of senior alternative programs in their schools. The WISE acronym now stands for Westchester's Pioneers in Individual Senior Experience.

One of the basic tenets of WISE Services is that each school must craft its own program. The WISE Services team merely makes suggestions, provides districts with information, and establishes a critical timeline for the implementation of the various stages of the project. Schools are encouraged to engage students, parents, teachers, community members, and administrators in the development process. The WISE team in each school maintains contact with representatives from WISE Services. The district pays a nominal fee to WISE Services for its guidance. The program has experienced overwhelming success.

Students who participate in the WISE Program receive high school credit for their work, which involves working on an individualized research project with a mentor. The amount of credit granted for participating varies from district to district. Some districts grant two credits in English and Social Studies, whereas other districts provide one English credit. The students are introduced to the WISE Program at the beginning of their senior year of high school when they begin to research their project, submit their proposals, and secure a mentor. Beginning on February 1, each student is released from certain classes to conduct the research, start regular meetings with their mentor, and work on their individualized project. The structure of these programs varies from district to district.

From its beginnings, the goals of the WISE Program have been similar to those of the Science Research Program. The 1980 WISE handbook outlined three major objectives of the program. The first was to promote personal and intellectual growth through increasing responsibility, improving student decision making, enhancing self-reliance, improving research skills, and conducting an in-depth study in an area of interest.[4]

The second objective of the program was to personalize the relationship between the student and the teacher through the establishment of a one-to-one mentor relationship, engaging in a cooperative research project, agreeing to direct and mutual accessibility, providing individualized instruction, increasing the rapport between mentor and student, and facilitating a mutual exchange of ideas throughout the learning experience.[5]

The third objective of the WISE Program was to improve the relationship between the student and the community through the use of community resources, community participation, and the promotion of student leadership within the community.[6]

The WISE Program provides each student with a unique and individualized learning experience during the senior year of high school. The Science Research Program and WISE initiative possess many of the same goals and themes. The WISE Program has an additional component because it involves community service. Involvement in the community is one of the main tenets of the third and final mentoring program included in this study, the Junior Firefighter Corps.

COMMUNITY-BASED MENTORING—INTERNSHIP PROGRAMS

The Junior Firefighter Corps is a community service program that has been established by volunteer fire departments in many suburban communities across the country. It provides students with exceptional experiential learning opportunities. Through volunteer fire departments, local residents dedicate countless hours to their communities and provide a vital service. The involvement of teenagers in these service-based programs provides students with the opportunity to give back to their communities. These programs differ slightly from the other two internship opportunities in this study because students are not required to develop a long-range, individualized project. The students also receive either civic internship or community service credit on their high school transcript. Involvement in this program might appear to be less academically rigorous than the previous two internship programs, but students are required to enroll in coursework to attain Firefighter 1 status. This coursework involves seventy-five hours of instruction. Individuals also have the option of pursuing Firefighter 2 status, which involves an additional forty-five hours of coursework. Whereas these community-based programs are treated differently by public schools, they were a vital component of our study and demonstrate the need to include mentoring and internship programs that meet the varied interests of all children.[7]

The purpose of the Junior Firefighter Corps is outlined in the program's standard operating procedure manual. The program seeks to stimulate interest and train qualified youth for volunteer fire service in their community. The program is open to any individual from fifteen to seventeen years of age who satisfactorily passes a background check, maintains a "C" average or better, meets residency requirements, has parental consent, obtains medical clearance, and attends the orientation meeting.[8]

Once the above criteria are met, the prospective students begin an eight-week probationary period during which they attend training sessions at the firehouse. The prospective junior firefighters are evaluated on their attendance, motivation, initiative, teamwork, attitude, professionalism, willingness to work, physical ability to perform basic fire department duties, and maturity. After a review of their performance during their probationary period, they are then either granted or denied admission to the junior corps.[9]

The members of the junior corps work closely with the adult volunteer firefighters. The students are permitted to perform certain acts during an actual emergency according to the amount of training and coursework they have completed. The academic component of this program is quite rigorous and certification requires an extensive time commitment. Because students who participate in this program do so by their choice, they are highly motivated and have a high level of interest in the program. Over the two-year period, positive adult-student relationships are fostered, and the students' efforts are embraced by the community.

STUDENT INTERNSHIPS—
A PHILOSOPHICAL INQUIRY

> It is in fact nothing short of a miracle that the modern methods of instruction have not yet entirely strangled the holy curiosity of inquiry; for this delicate little plant, aside from stimulation, stands mainly in need of freedom; without this it goes to wrack and ruin without fail.
>
> —Albert Einstein[10]

There is increasing interest by educators in new opportunities for mentoring and internship programs that can provide students with effective experiential learning opportunities. "Experiential learning" has been defined as "when participants are fully involved, when the lessons are clearly relevant to the participants, when individuals develop a sense of responsibility for their own learning, and when the learning environment is flexible, responsive to the participant's immediate needs."[11]

The three mentoring/internship programs that we examined in this study contain all of these necessary components to an effective experiential learning program. With increased pressure exerted by the current standards movement, however, educational leaders are somewhat resistant to stray from traditional pedagogical practices. Several renowned experts in the education field have observed that traditional education can stifle the development of the total adolescent.[12] Paulo Freire was one of these philosophers, and A. Darder offered this compelling summary of Freire's views on this phenomenon of a rigid status quo within the educational bureaucracy:

He wrote of the fear of freedom that afflicts us, a fear predicated on prescriptive relationships between those who rule (state education departments, teachers) and those who are expected to follow (teachers, students). As critical educators, he urged us to question carefully our ideological beliefs and pedagogical intentions and to take note of our adherence to the status quo. . . . It is true that the concrete execution of teaching practice takes place within the localized boundaries of the classroom. But to remain solely within the confines of those four walls in one's analysis or interpretation of what constitutes the lives of students and teachers is naively to refuse to acknowledge the interdependent nature of all existence.[13]

While we want children to develop strong critical thinking skills that ready them for success in a complex world, traditional education offered within the four walls of public schools may not provide the foundation they need for the transition to adult life, including the transition to college.[14]

The philosophical underpinnings of experiential learning have been addressed by a number of other respected philosophers. They cite the importance of varying a child's learning experience. Experiential learning also gives students the opportunity to enhance many personal attributes by giving them greater autonomy and responsibility, allowing them to engage in self-directed learning and exposing them to the real world and academic freedom. Carl Rogers placed great importance on helping students develop the skills to direct their own learning:

> A way must be found to develop a climate in the system in which the focus is not upon teaching, but upon the facilitation of self-directed learning. Only then can we develop a creative individual who is open to all of his experience; aware of it and accepting it, and continually in the process of changing. And only this way, I believe, can we bring about the creative organization, which will also be continually in the process of changing.[15]

Educational leaders need to reflect and ask challenging questions regarding the creativity of their own educational organizations. When we become so driven by mandates and regulations, creativity can be easily sacrificed.

Each of the programs we studied requires the participants to work independently, thus promoting autonomy. Each program fosters positive relationships between students and mentors or adults involved in the program, and each requires students to engage in extensive coursework or relevant research relating to their project.

When students transition from high school to college, they experience a significant increase in autonomy and are required to work independently. The students who participated in these school-based mentoring programs were given an opportunity to be autonomous and responsible for their time management while they were still in high school. They had the opportunity to work independently to meet deadlines. The mentor in these programs served to monitor progress, advise students, and provide an opportunity for students to reflect on their progress. The students had the opportunity to develop these skills while still living at home and relying on their established support systems.

The second common goal of these mentoring and internship programs is for students to develop positive working relationships with a mentor or adults involved in the program. Earlier, we discussed the detrimental effect of the adolescent society that our schools foster and encourage. When students depart from that environment for a portion of their high school experience, they are forced to grow and mature and develop many of the adult skills they will need to make a successful transition to college. One writer described the challenge confronting our schools this way:

> Seniors are young adults, not children. By January, they are ready to do something different and find out what adult life has in store for

them. . . . Send these good kids out into career-related internships or community service projects that they choose. . . . Faculty members could shift from hectoring the catatonic to advising the eager on where they should intern.[16]

The relationship between the student and adult mentor is critical to the success of internship programs. Educational leaders and mentors in these programs must introduce the total experience to the student by outlining course expectations, establishing levels of involvement, encouraging openness and risk taking, and agreeing upon a system of dynamic feedback.[17]

Any innovation in education produces detractors. Some critics of mentoring and internship programs claim there is a lack of academic rigor because learning is not measured in traditional ways, such as through tests. This criticism is not a new phenomenon:

> It is ironic that so many traditional educators malign critical forms of education that are based on Freire's work as impractical or lacking academic rigor. Nothing could be further from the truth. . . . This is a living practice that is composed of relevant pedagogical actions within schools and communities that stimulate students' critical intellectual engagement with their world.[18]

Advocates of experiential learning programs are well aware of this criticism and emphasize that academic rigor must be a priority in any internship or mentoring programs. One scholar said internships should be more rigorous than high school classes: "Why not make that taste of college more real by offering less classroom contact time and more material to master. Then we could see if these seniors really are ready for college's pace."[19]

School districts across the country are entertaining the implementation of experiential learning programs during the senior year of high school "to stimulate students' critical intellectual engagement with their world."[20] Extensive research has identified severe problems with the senior year of high school, including the lack of academic achievement by students and the lack of their connection to the real world. Researchers have indicated that this is an institutional problem because there is such a significant disconnect between secondary and postsecondary institutions: "High school seniors who take a break from tough academic courses are reacting rationally to a K–12 system and a college admissions process that provide few incentives for students to work hard during their senior year."[21]

Instead of perpetuating a system that reduces the academic demands placed on high school seniors, we must create opportunities for them to engage in challenging learning experiences outside the classroom and to start to build the foundation they will need to make the transition from high school to college. There is no question that experiential learning programs help students prepare for this important transition.

Philosophers who support nontraditional educational practices may be viewed as extremists by those educators who defend the status quo, and resist innovation, including experiential learning opportunities. One scholar wrote that the growing movement toward more standardized testing undermines educational innovation:

> The strong movement within this country to mandate testing of children's learning in public schools could well discourage activities that foster thinking. State assessment programs are already detractors from those activities, as teachers are understandably led to prepare students for tests. And those tests focus largely on learned facts, a far cry from measuring quality education, with its emphasis on thinking and problem solving as well as knowledge.[22]

It is easy to stay within our comfort zone, to send our children to schools that look and act like the schools we attended and our parents attended. Over two centuries ago, Rousseau challenged us to recognize the nature of true learning:

> Let the senses be the only guide for the first workings of reason. No book but the world, no teaching but that of fact. The child who

reads ceases to think, he only reads. He is acquiring words not knowledge. Teach your scholar to observe the phenomena of nature; you will soon rouse his curiosity, but if you would have it grow, do not be in too great a hurry to satisfy his curiosity. Put the problems before him and let him solve the problems himself. . . . Let him not be taught science, let him discover it. If you ever substitute authority for reason he will cease to reason.[23]

Dewey reminded us of the importance of offering students unique learning experiences to help them develop into critical thinkers:

> Processes of instruction are unified in the degree in which they center in the production of good habits of thinking. . . . The important thing is that thinking is the method of an educative experience. The essentials of method are therefore identical with the essentials of reflection. They are first that the pupil have a genuine situation of experience— that there be a continuous activity in which he is interested for its own sake . . . that a genuine problem develop within this situation as a stimulus of thought . . . that suggested solutions occur to him which he shall be responsible for developing in an orderly way . . . that he have opportunity and occasion to test his ideas by application, to make their meaning clear and to discover for himself their validity.[24]

Dewey spoke of the need to challenge students with the "genuine situation of experience" in order to learn how to think and problem solve, and he stressed the importance of the student's interest in the work at hand. These are fundamental tenets of the mentoring and internship movement: real experiences help students identify and pursue their interests and are essential to learning.

NOTES

1. D. Littky and S. Grabelle, *The Big Picture: Education Is Everyone's Business* (Alexandria, VA: Association for Supervision and Curriculum Development, 2004).
2. Littky and Grabelle, *The Big Picture*, 122.
3. Littky and Grabelle, *The Big Picture*, 124.

4. T. Abramson and V. Leviatin, *Woodlands Individualized Senior Experience Manual* (Greenburgh, NY: Greenburgh Central School District No. 7, 1980).

5. Abramson and Leviatin, *Woodlands Individualized Senior Experience Manual*.

6. Abramson and Leviatin, *Woodlands Individualized Senior Experience Manual*.

7. Yorktown Heights Fire Department (Y.H.F.D.), *Yorktown Heights Fire Department: Junior Corps Standard Operating Guidelines* (Yorktown Heights, NY: author, 2005).

8. Y.H.F.D., *Yorktown Heights Fire Department*.

9. Y.H.F.D., *Yorktown Heights Fire Department*.

10. C. R. Rogers and H. Freiberg, *Freedom to Learn* (Columbus, OH: Merrill, 1994), ix.

11. G. Walter and S. Marks, *Experiential Learning and Change* (New York: John Wiley, 1981), 2.

12. P. Freire, *Pedagogy of Hope* (New York: Continuum, 1994).

13. A. Darder, *Reinventing Paulo Freire* (Boulder, CO: Westview, 2002), 37, 83.

14. D. Stern, "Career Academies and High School Reform Before, During, and After the School-to-Work Movement. Spotlight on Student Success" (Washington, DC: Office of Educational Research and Improvement, 2001).

15. C. R. Rogers, *Freedom to Learn* (Columbus, OH: Merrill, 1969), 304.

16. C. Teare, "Cut Senior Year in Half," *Education Week* 25, no. 6:32.

17. Walter and Marks, *Experiential Learning and Change*.

18. Darder, *Reinventing Paulo Freire*, 84.

19. Teare, "Cut Senior Year in Half," 32.

20. Darder, *Reinventing Paulo Freire*, 84.

21. M. Kirst and A. Venezia, *From High School to College: Improving Opportunities for Success in Postsecondary Education* (San Francisco: Jossey-Bass, 2004), 302.

22. M. Schwebel, *Remaking America's Three School Systems* (Lanham, MD: Scarecrow, 2003), 60.

23. J. J. Rousseau, *Emile* (London: Aldine, 1969), 131.

24. J. Dewey, *Democracy and Education* (New York: The Free Press, 1944).

5

NINE STORIES FROM THE FIELD

Extensive research and interviews are the basis for the findings and recommendations made in this book. The nine students who shared their experiences and reflections with us were either enrolled in college or had recently graduated at the time of the interviews in the spring of 2006. Each of these students participated in an internship program while in high school.

The nine participants represent the ethnic and racial diversity of the student body in public education today. In the area of academic achievement, these students were successful in high school, had a positive internship experience, and continued their success in college. These success stories give us important insights into the significance of a successful internship program through the eyes of the participant.

The interview process provided us with valuable data about each student's high school experience, family life, and personal growth. These are their stories. Identifying information has been changed to protect their privacy.

WILLIAM

William is a Caucasian male who was a senior at a state university during the research period. William participated in the Science Research Program at Wayne High School. He conducted a research project investigating the West Nile virus, a biological phenomenon that was impacting a majority of the communities in the tristate area of New York, New Jersey, and Connecticut. He conducted his research in a laboratory setting off school grounds over a two-year period. William received college credit for his internship program and competed in several local and regional science research competitions. William was a B+ to A student in high school, where he participated in cross-country and described himself as "an all around student in good standing." He considered himself "the quiet type, never one of the more popular kids, I had friends amongst the more academic crowd."

William's parents divorced while William was in high school. His parents both had extensive careers working in various retail stores for nearly twenty-five years. William currently lives with his mother and grandmother when he is not away at school. He works part-time to support himself and is paying his own way through college. William is an English major and plans to graduate in May 2006. William said he feels that he has been successful in college and said, "I figure I'm among the average, the usual college senior. I get my work done; I think I have a lot of aptitude for the work force. So far I would qualify myself as a success."

DEBBIE

Debbie is a Caucasian female who was born in Russia and started her public education in New York State, where she was eligible for English as a Second Language (ESL) support in the first grade. Debbie was an excellent student in high school and received a full scholarship to a prestigious engineering school in a major metropolitan area. She transferred to an honors college in a southern state where she was a senior at the time this study was conducted. When asked about her transfer to another school, she responded, "It was probably one of the best choices I've ever made to come down to the honors college. I made it for the wrong reason; I was in a relationship that didn't work out. But I'm inexplicably happy coming down here because the environment is more conducive to learning."

Debbie participated in the science research program in South High School. She participated in the program for two years and received college credit for her coursework. She conducted her research in the field of AIDS, where she studied the synergy between various HIV medicines that were new to the market.

She said that she was not outgoing in high school, although she had a "diverse group of friends." She also admitted, "I was very good at doing the bare minimum to do the best I could and do well. I graduated in the Honor Society and received a full scholarship."

Debbie's mother and father are both engineers. She classified herself as "middle class" and worked several part-time jobs throughout her high school years. Debbie reported that she feels she is extremely successful, has high expectations for herself academically, and sees herself going to medical school because "what's better than going to medical school and receiving an MD, PhD to vouch for you saying that you did well."

RHAMI

Rhami was born in India and moved to this country prior to his formal schooling years. He was the valedictorian of his high school and received a full scholarship to a prestigious university in a major metropolitan area. Rhami participated in the Science Research

Program in his high school and conducted his research at a renowned school of medicine, where he worked with a full-time research team. Rhami conducted stem cell development research and participated in local, regional, and national competitions through the Science Research Program.

Reflecting back on his high school years, Rhami described himself as a "very motivated student. I did very well academically. . . . High school had always been more of a breeze. . . . Socially I think I was a bit of an introvert at times and so socially I had a small and close group of friends that I spent most of my time with."

Rhami said that when he began college, "it was more challenging than I had anticipated and that lasted effectively for one semester, and so I worked harder and it became a breeze again." Rhami continues to experience success in the corporate world working as a business consultant for a major firm based in the Atlanta area.

Rhami's father is a computer consultant, and his mother is an accountant. Rhami's family lived in a northern suburb of a major metropolitan area, and he described his socioeconomic status as middle- to upper-middle class.

ANN

Ann is a Caucasian female who is a recent graduate from an excellent university in a major metropolitan area. Ann participated in the WISE Internship Program during her senior year of high school. Her internship program placed her in the middle of New York City's Broadway theater district, one of the most renowned in the world. A few of her internship experiences included working in the theater with actors performing their readings, assisting in the sound and lighting booths, observing understudy rehearsals, and sitting in on playwrights creating scenes for upcoming plays.

Ann was the salutatorian for her high school graduating class. When asked to describe her academic performance in high school, she said, "Basically I was an honors student, I took some A.P. classes, and I did well in everything that I did." When asked about the social aspects of high school, she stated, "I had a group of friends that came together my freshman year. . . . We hung out in the art room, originally we were all on the yearbook staff and we were kind of drawn to the arts. . . . We would do the plays together. . . . At times we seemed different from the rest of the school. . . . They would ridicule us. . . . We got through it because we had each other."

Ann lived at home with her mother and older brother. Her parents divorced when she was very young, partially due to her father's alcoholism and his inability to maintain steady employment. The mother is a language teacher in a nearby school district.

Two years ago, during her undergraduate studies, Ann realized that she was no longer interested in pursuing a career in drama. She said she discovered that she "wanted to do something a little more literary and less performing." She is currently pursuing her master's degree in library science and plans to become a children's librarian "because I love children's literature. . . . I want to incorporate theatre into the idea of encouraging children to become early readers." She has always considered herself successful academically and continues to be an excellent student.

JAMES

James is an African-American male who attends a prestigious college in a major metropolitan area. James participated in the WISE Internship Program during his senior year of high school when he volunteered at a gay and lesbian youth organization in a nearby city. As a gay adolescent, James felt the desire to contribute to the rights of gay and lesbian students in the communities surrounding his high school. When asked why he chose this specific internship, he stated, "I knew I wanted to do something having to do with gay rights just because it's my life. . . . I had a personal dedication to a certain project. I became very, very focused."

When asked about his academic achievement in high school James replied, "I was an A student pretty much all my life. . . . I love school, I absolutely loved high school and I loved excelling in it. . . . I was part of the National Honor Society, Key Club, Drama Club, Music Honors Society, Yearbook Staff, and the literary magazine." Socially, James described himself as "socially active, keeping a small group of friends with which they did a lot of things all the time."

James lives with his mother, his maternal grandparents, and his younger brother. His grandparents were both teachers at the high school James attended. His grandmother also held an important position in local government while his grandfather currently is a trainer who works with patients who are receiving rehabilitation for Parkinson's disease. His mother is a school psychologist in a nearby district. James considered his family to be middle- to upper-middle class and lived a comfortable life in a northern suburb of a major metropolitan area.

TANYA

Tanya is a black female who is a recent immigrant from Haiti. Tanya came to the United States during her junior year of high school and immediately achieved academic success. At the time of this study, she was a sophomore at a small liberal arts college in a northern suburb of a major metropolitan area. Tanya participated in the WISE Internship Program in high school, where she served as a volunteer at a school specifically designed to meet the needs of children with severe autism and Down's syndrome. One of Tanya's personal reflections regarding her decision to work with these children was that "in Haiti you're not exposed to autistic or Down's syndrome children. . . . Because we don't have that in Haiti, we don't care for people who are autistic or Down's syndrome." This experience confirmed Tanya's passion for working in this area and supported her decision to pursue her degree in developmental psychology in order to work with disabled children.

When asked about her brief tenure in an American high school she said, "I had a 4.0 GPA, I was working very hard, I was involved in different clubs, doing extracurricular activities and I was pretty social." Her academic success and adjustment to college have been exceptional: "I have a lot of friends. Right now I am currently sitting on a 3.7 GPA and I'm involved in everything. I am a resident assistant, an orientation leader, involved in student government, and I have my own radio show. I'm doing pretty good."

Tanya lived with her mother all of her life until moving to the United States. Her father is deceased. She currently lives with her great uncle (her grandfather's brother), who is a custodial worker at a nursing home. In Haiti, she described her socioeconomic status as "high class," whereas her aunt and uncle here in America would be considered "middle or working class."

HARRY

Harry is a Caucasian male who was a member of the Junior Firefighter Corps in his town during high school. Harry received community service credit in high school for his involvement in the junior corps and received several nominal scholarships upon graduation from high school for his contributions to his local community. Harry was a junior at a local liberal arts college and commuted to school at the time this research was conducted.

Harry classified himself as an average student in high school. He reported that "academically my grades were okay, my SAT scores were average, I went to every class. . . . Socially, I talked to everyone, I played football and baseball, I was diverse.... I talked to everyone, got along with everyone."

Harry is an only child and lives with his mother and father. His father sells auto parts at a local store, and Harry said he considers himself "middle class." Harry grew up in a middle-class community where he continues to be active as a volunteer firefighter when he is not attending school or coaching a local little league team.

Harry said that he has made a successful transition to college. He indicated that he "adjusted pretty well" and that "academically I knew it was going to be a step up from high school." He said his college "prepares you pretty well" and provided freshman orientation and a required seminar to assist in the adjustment to college. He said that he knew "there was going to be more work and that was one of the challenges that I overcame."

TONY

Tony was involved in the Junior Firefighter Corps in high school and received community service credit for his contributions to his local community. At the time of this research, Tony was a junior and lived on campus at a liberal arts college approximately thirty-five miles from his parents' home. Tony transferred to his current college after attending a different college in a neighboring state during his freshman year. Tony said that during his first year at the other college, "I really didn't adjust well. I drank a lot of beer. Once I transferred to my new school, I found myself very well adjusted. I was a lot more happy." Tony maintained approximately a 3.5 GPA during his college studies.

Tony recalled that in his high school years "I was pretty much an average student, maybe a C+ or B average. I was known as an athlete, I played hockey. I really wasn't much of a studier.... I was very social."

Tony's' father has owned a local plumbing company for twenty-seven years. Tony has been working part-time for his father since he was about fourteen years old. Tony's mother also works in the family business as a secretary. His older brother also works for his father and is one of the foremen. Tony's parents met each other in high school in a neighboring town before settling into their current community and establishing their successful family business.

PETER

Peter participated in the Junior Firefighter Corps in a neighboring town during high school and received community service credit for his commitment to the volunteer fire department. Peter was a sophomore in college at the time of this study, attending a private university outside a metropolitan area in upstate New York. He carried a double major in political science and the creative arts with a concentration in theater.

Peter grew up in a suburban community where his father practiced law and his mother worked as a physical therapy assistant in a nearby town. Peter has two younger brothers and although Peter worked to pay for his college tuition, he classified his family's socioeconomic status as "comfortable."

Peter shared interesting insight into his high school years. He said that he was a "pretty good student, with an 87 or 88 average. . . . Having a learning disability required me to become an advocate at an early age. . . . I was very busy in high school; I worked in the theatre, swam for our school team, participated in the Boy Scouts and participated in an extensive internship program. . . . I hung out with the athletes and theater kids. . . . Pretty much everyone."

As a sophomore in college, Peter shared his feelings regarding his success in postsecondary education: "I'm definitely struggling in some classes, but I know I'm putting forth the best I can and I'm about a 3.0 student. . . . So overall I'm pretty successful, doing a good job, learning a lot." Peter's candor provided a vivid picture of how some students struggle with academics in postsecondary education but ultimately manage to be successful.

6

STUDENT INTERNSHIPS: SHAPING THE HIGH SCHOOL EXPERIENCE

While traditional schooling places students in the role of passive learners for thirteen years, the experiential learning that is inherent in an internship program requires real learning in the real world.

In this chapter you will hear the genuine and authentic reflections of nine special individuals. Collectively, they validate the need and the importance of the internship experience. Their candor and honesty may remind you of an adolescent you know, whether it be your own child, a neighbor, relative, or acquaintance. Their stories are powerful, and the qualities and personal growth that they attribute to their internship experience provided a solid foundation to meet the challenges of postsecondary education, allowing them to find their own portal to personal success and growth.

The philosophical underpinnings of experiential learning were discussed in chapter 4. The reflections and insights of these students, however, reveal that their internship experiences were intense and vivid learning experiences in which they were not only challenged intellectually but had the chance to grow and develop personal attributes that contributed to their high school and college experiences.

The three internship programs in this study provided the students with a sense of independence and achievement, the opportunity to develop and pursue a passion, and a unique learning experience. The students all reflected back on their respective programs and described how the programs contributed to their high school experience and to their successful transition to college.

The students, and the internships they undertook, are diverse. But despite these variables, common themes emerged regarding the ways in which these experiential learning opportunities contributed to their individual development and helped them develop attributes necessary for success in college and beyond.

INDEPENDENCE

All the students observed a stark contrast between their traditional high school classes and the independence they experienced during their internship programs. They reflected on the individual growth that this independence fostered and the ways in which it prepared them for the academic, social, and emotional challenges of postsecondary education.

Several of the respondents were openly critical of certain characteristics of traditional education. Debbie observed, "An A or an A– on a report card is pretty much the same thing. What is it going to mean. . . . It's not going to make that much of a difference. . . . I look good on paper." Her comments reflect the disconnect that high school students can experience between the meaning of their studies and whether they are actually benefiting from what they are learning. As a recent immigrant, Tanya was not overly impressed with the public education system in the United States and said, "In Haiti, you get a lot of work. . . . Like going from Haiti to high school here was actually easy, I don't think the work load was tough in high school." Unlike Debbie and Tanya, some respondents classified themselves as average high school students. Yet these students,

Harry and Tony, also were unimpressed at times with the traditional schooling they experienced. Harry unenthusiastically recalled that "my grades were okay," and Tony recounted, "I really wasn't much of a studier" and "I was pretty much an average student."

Throughout the study the respondents reminded us how they valued the opportunity to participate in an internship program while in high school. Ann felt strongly that the WISE Program promoted independence:

> In a big way I felt independent in the [internship] program.... You get to choose what it is going to be. You have to choose your own topic.... There is an array of things in the world and you choose the one that you are interested in, something that you want to test out for whatever the reason and you want to pursue it.... So just given the power to make that decision is big. I mean that's a great thing.

This sentiment about the powerful nature of an independent learning experience was echoed by William, who participated in the science research program in high school. William said that "in terms of independence, all of my work was pretty much done on my own accord. I designed my own study, did my own research, all of which was self-motivated. College work follows the same sort of thing; you have to do your own work. During the internship, however, someone is there to help you along." Rhami also participated in the Science Research Program, and he recalled, "The defining moment and challenge really leads me to interpret that the freedom you're given challenges your ability to organize that freedom and to be self-motivated to continue to push for something that as a high-school student is so abstract that you really can't get your hands on it, but still you find the motivation to do so."

The common thread of the importance of independence ran through the experiences of all the respondents, regardless of which internship they pursued. Harry stated that the Junior Firefighter Corps "definitely opened up a whole new spectrum, because it puts more responsibility and makes kids think, putting them in critical situations." The independent nature of internship programs clearly puts young adults in different environments and entrusts them with newfound autonomy. For James, the internship opened up a new world:

> Fantastic, actually it was great. You'd just hop in your car and drive off, not be on school grounds and doing something that really mattered. You know, instead of shit. It was great to have an opportunity to be on my own and develop human issues and impart my knowledge and then write about it. So, it was really great to have that independence. I think I should have done more with it. It was great.

In today's public education system there are limited opportunities for students to experience this degree of independence and to strive toward goals while working independently on a school project. As a recent immigrant to this country, Tanya wanted to experience the academic freedom of an internship experience:

> I wanted to end my high school career differently. I did not want to take regular English class just for the sake of it, and WISE was a way for me to explore everything and I had a chance of working in a field that I was interested in, which is psychology, so I thought it was a good opportunity, a very unusual way of ending high school. . . . It made me very independent. . . . You're on your own. . . . It's a wake up call, welcome to reality.

Debbie worked endless hours in the laboratory conducting AIDS research. She said the independence she experienced was infused with the nature of science research:

> It's getting your data to fit, getting your data to work, coming up with new ideas and you have to work for it, it's not like something that's handed to you because of twenty minutes of work. It's something that you really have to research, I mean that's what it is, it's re-

search. It's the pursuit of knowledge and you really have to, in order to get any results, put everything into it. . . . In this pursuit you're trying to figure it out and you work much harder to figure it out because there's no right answer, it's not like school. . . . There is no right answer, there is no combination that will save someone's life in this type of research because we don't know enough about it, and we're searching for it.

For Debbie, the experience of working independently within an internship program was personal and passionate. Tony also discussed the independence he felt learning in an environment that he personally chose, as well as the hands-on nature of his internship experience, when he reported, "First of all it was hands-on and it was better for me because I was more of a hands-on learner anyway, but it was more interesting, you could ask more questions, and there wasn't just one teacher the whole time. Some of the other guys would sit in on the training and put in their two cents if they wanted to, so you'd get different ideas and views on how to do something."

The independent nature of learning in a hands-on environment away from a traditional classroom was appealing to Tony, who placed a priority on his work at his internship:

Yeah, definitely sometimes I put that before school because I wasn't really a school person, but that was just more interesting to me, of course, the job as a fireman so it's probably going to be more interesting to most people, yeah at times I definitely put more time in there because there are things like the fundraisers and such.

The respondents clearly articulated their memories of the academic freedom they experienced through their participation in an internship program. These students were provided with the opportunity to learn independently, a challenge that is frequently not available or minimal in traditional educational environments.

Whereas each of the programs provided the participants with some form of independence, there were some differences due to the individual nature of each internship. The main contrast was between the community service programs and the other internship experiences, which took the individuals farther away from their schools, communities, and homes. As mentioned in the brief biographies, the students who participated in the community service programs were average students in high school who developed a true camaraderie in the firehouse. Harry reported, "Ever since I was little I always wanted to be a fireman. All my relatives are firemen and everything, so I was kind of around the firehouse a lot, family parties and everything, so it just kind of grew on me. . . . It just made me think more and get a better sense and like my community." Tony recalled the same feelings when he spoke of the "camaraderie, sticking up for one another. Around here when something happens, we're all there for each other." Although it may appear that these students are not experiencing an independent learning experience, underlying their strong sense of family and camaraderie is their clear perception that they were able to choose this opportunity to learn in an environment independent of their traditional schooling.

The experiences placed many different faces on the term "independence." The sense of independence felt by James as he drove off campus to follow his passion and promote gay rights is quite different from Rhami, who recalled the challenge as an "ambiguous undertaking, you're off researching something you've never heard of." Yet while they experienced the sense of independence in different ways, that autonomy provided each student with a unique, powerful learning experience.

ACHIEVEMENT

All of the students reported they felt a sense of achievement or accomplishment in their high school internship experience. Student achievement is the foundation of public education, and it is important to recognize that student achievement comes in many forms, not merely quantitative data that can be scored with traditional assessment strategies. The internship programs in this study required the students to conduct scientific research, commit to extensive hours of community service, enroll in challenging courses outside of high school, or prepare detailed exit projects and final presentations. School districts across the country are offering internship opportunities that are extremely demanding. The participants felt a great sense of pride and accomplishment as a result of the work they did through their internship programs.

Several of the internship programs provided the participants with an opportunity to make a meaningful societal contribution. As an activist for gay rights, James spoke of the sense of accomplishment and empowerment he experienced from "going to different schools and talking about making school safer for gay and lesbian students, and teachers fueled my passion for political and social reform in New York as well as America in general. Lobbying in Albany and talking to senators made me aware of my power as a constituent. Being a part of a greater whole made me realize how important it is to fight for what you believe in and to encourage others to fight for civil rights."

In the field of AIDS research, Debbie echoed similar feelings when she stated, "When you know that there's something that's going to come out of what you're doing, or there could come out based on your efforts, your driving force increases so much, because you know that this could change someone's life, you know that in my case, my research in HIV could be used and implemented in clinical trials and it could help someone live a better life, a longer life."

The basic tenet of the Junior Firefighter Corps obviously centers on community service. Harry said the desire to work for his community motivated him because, "I want to do it to better myself and better the community with helping and serving people." The three participants from the community service programs felt very close ties to their community. Tony remembered that his time spent in the firehouse "gave me somewhere to go. . . . I hung out at the firehouse. . . . It gave me something to do and the feeling that I'm doing something right. . . . You want to know the things that are going to help you be safe and help somebody else." Peter said the experience fulfilled a childhood dream, "Since I was like one year old, the first toys I had were fire trucks. . . . I was very much into it. . . . I love every aspect of it. . . . It reminded me a lot of my family, everyone was always close. . . . I'm really interested in it. . . . Just helping people."

Many of the internship programs require a portfolio and a presentation at the end of the school year highlighting the internship program, which was viewed as a major achievement by several of the participants. All of the students who participated in the WISE Program vividly recalled this challenging accomplishment. Ann said that she was required to "speak with leaders in my field on a regular basis, and then present my findings in a forty-minute presentation at the end of the program." Ann reported that this experience strengthened her self-confidence and her ability to clearly articulate thoughts. Tanya vividly recounted the challenge she faced in her internship experience: "Then I had to give a presentation in front of all those people and talking about a subject that is close to your heart, it was a really good experience, but at first I was nervous about the presentation, but as I was talking I didn't even remember who was looking because I was talking about something I loved." It is obvious that her internship experience and final presentation were genuine learning experiences that helped her begin to acquire essential life skills.

The third respondent who participated in the WISE Program, James, made many presentations throughout his internship when he visited public high schools to speak to students regarding gay rights. In addition to learning to become an advocate by being one, James said he felt that he made great strides in the area of public speaking and stated, "It helped my public speaking quite a bit. I was never afraid of public speaking, but it is a different thing to perform than to get up in front of people and talk about your life, your personal hardships, what happened to you and how to apply that to other people and how to make a difference. . . . I believe WISE helped me better express myself."

The respondents who participated in the Science Research Program expressed pride in their accomplishments and achievements. The science research program includes countless hours conducting research and competing in regional and national competitions. William detailed the rigorous nature of his research project, which started with "hours of hands-on work. . . . Charting and calculating my data. . . . Doing a statistical analysis. . . . And then later on going to competitions and developing my public speaking ability." Debbie's experience was similar, and she recalled her growth and accomplishments in the area of public speaking and learning to present her data:

> Actually, I remember the first time I presented PowerPoint. It was at JSHS [Junior Science and Humanities Symposium] and I wanted to die. I stuttered and I had no confidence, I was unsure and repetitive, oh, I read off my notes and it was a miserable experience, absolutely miserable. . . . That was one experience that I kind of drilled in the back of my head that I never want to have happen again.
>
> So, I had to present again later on in tri-county, where I moved on as a semi-finalist. My presentation went so smoothly I didn't know it was me presenting. As for ISEF [Intel Science Talent Search], I never really had a problem presenting one on one, or one, two or three people, because I never had that pressure. I felt like a conversationalist, and as a conversationalist I excelled. I think that was my favorite part of ISEF, I liked convincing people; I was able to sell my project, which is probably the most important aspect of life and science research.

Debbie recognized that these formidable accomplishments in high school had a significant impact on her growth as a person. The extensive nature of her internship program provided her with many opportunities to be successful and post notable achievements. Rhami said he felt the same sense of achievement, and he recalled, "I would say it was almost like one big adventure. . . . I tend to like to do well. . . . I was really intimidated by some folks who obviously were better prepared. . . . I had won the Regional competition and I was already in Detroit, which in itself was a great accomplishment."

All of the respondents who participated in the Science Research Program indicated that they felt a great sense of accomplishment, and in fact this was shared by all the participants in this study. However, the data reveals that the actual achievements can differ greatly according to the individual and the internship in which they chose to participate. The more academically driven student tended to look at the internship as an opportunity to delve into research and develop higher order thinking skills over the course of several years. The more average student with close community ties saw the internship experience as an opportunity to give back to his community and become a part of a close-knit fraternity of firefighters. The WISE Program offered a variety of opportunities, ranging from working with disabled children to following a personal dream or passion such as working in the theater or advocating for gay rights.

The internship experiences also gave these students an opportunity to discover, develop, and pursue a personal passion. In this regard, these adolescents were provided an opportunity that is rare in traditional public education.

PASSION

Throughout the data collection process, several of the respondents spoke about experiencing a "passion" for the work they did during their internship experience. During the course of the research, the students had repeated opportunities to provide in-depth responses describing their experiences. The respondents continually reminded us of the personal nature of their internship experience, and they recalled the drive and passion they felt throughout their experience. This common thread of discovery and pursuit of a passion is an extremely important aspect of student internship programs. In order for a high school student to pursue an experiential learning opportunity with the vigor necessary to make the experience exceptional, the program must be in an area that is close to the individual's heart. James remembered:

> Going to different schools and talking about making school safer for gay and lesbian students and teachers fueled my passion for political and social reform in New York as well as America in general. Lobbying in Albany and talking to senators made me aware of my power as a constituent. Being a part of a greater whole made me realize how important it is to fight for what you believe in and to encourage others to fight for civil rights.

James was fortunate to participate in an internship for which he possessed such passion. In the second interview, he continued to recall his enthusiasm, "I jumped right in, I was thrilled. . . . From the time they let me in I went in head first. . . . I believe in it so much. . . . I can do this to help out and I will."

Several of the respondents experienced the same passion for the work in their experiential learning opportunities. The junior firefighters spoke about the intensity of the brotherhood that develops in the firehouse and Peter recalled, "I never really understood it until I joined. You always heard about the brotherhood, but you're going out putting your life on the line and I would trust everyone in that firehouse. I had a couple of experiences where things went wrong. I fell through the floor and another kid my age grabbed me before I went all the way through. I would go anywhere with them. I trust them like my brothers." Harry reported that "camaraderie is the number one thing that keeps everyone together." Tony said the experience "strengthened my values, it made me realize what type of person I was and it made me value friendship and family."

Debbie recalled the passion that she developed for her work during her Science Research Internship. She spent countless hours in the lab in a quest for answers, and she said, "I am one of those people who likes to see progress, I like seeing change, and I like being aware of the change that I affect.... To produce some triple cocktail that a person with HIV is now going to be able to take and decrease the chance of virus mutation and increase their life expectancy. It was amazing to see that I was a piece of that."

As part of her WISE Internship, Ann felt that she was provided an opportunity to explore her creative ability through the experience of writing a short story, which helped her discover more about how to pursue what she loves:

> The biggest way in which WISE affected my values and beliefs was in validating for me that creative pursuits are just as valuable and have just as much worth as other kinds of pursuits. Creating and making the time to do what you love is important and necessary—I realized this when I decided I would write a short play as part of my project, rather than simply going to a theatre-related internship once or twice a week. This is a belief I hold to this day, and without WISE to really give it real-world validity, I am not sure I would have continued to feel this way about the act of creating past the insulated world of high school.

Rhami revealed strong emotions and said he learned some valuable life lessons when working in the laboratory: "I learned exactly what drives me and how I can succeed.... I learned how to work with people in a work environment.... We tend to put them [doctors and professionals] on a pedestal." Rhami said the experience allowed him to "humanize" the professionals he worked with because he got to know many of them as "real people" and to see "not only the work they did, but how they engaged with each other at work." He said these connections he was able to make in turn "made the experience much more real and more tangible for me." While Rhami did not articulate the term "passion," he did clearly recall his internship experience as one that touched him in a deeply personal way, teaching him essential information about his own drive to succeed and the work world in which he would eventually take his place. These are basic components of the pursuit of one's passion.

William also recalled certain aspects of his internship experience that were quite similar to Rhami's experience. He also spent countless hours in a laboratory setting, and he found that "overall, it was a lot different than the rest of my other courses. I mean obviously it was an independent program, you obviously did a lot more. It was overall a really positive experience for me. . . . It was what I wanted to learn about." William's individual drive and his desire to contribute to the field of knowledge regarding the West Nile virus were evident in his passion for his science research project.

Tanya reminded us of a vital aspect of her internship experience when she reflected on her presentation: "Then I had to give a presentation in front of all those people and talking about a subject that is close to your heart, it was a really good experience, but at first I was nervous about the presentation, but as I was talking I didn't even remember who was looking because I was talking about something I loved." It is obvious that her internship experience and final presentation were genuine learning experiences. When she said that the experience was "close to her heart and something I loved," it is clear that this adolescent possessed a genuine passion for working with disabled children.

UNIQUENESS

Individual learning experiences inherently possess a certain level of "uniqueness." Each of the respondents discussed certain novel aspects of their internship program and how the experience was unique. After years of traditional schooling, the students embraced the opportunity to participate in an internship program of their choice. Freed from the shackles of public education, each participant was able to create their own independent learning experience under the tutelage of their mentor and make their mark on a certain aspect of society. The passion previously discussed was clearly fostered by the unique nature of the internship programs, which were new and exciting experiences for the majority of the study participants.

As a gay rights activist, James viewed his research project as an opportunity to accomplish certain goals before becoming immersed in his pursuit of a professional acting career. The unique nature of his internship experience is reflected in his own recollection of how he viewed the opportunity: "I chose it because I knew I was going into college for drama, that I probably wouldn't have a lot of time to work on this, which was my other passion, so I decided what better time to give this a shot." James also revealed the importance of another vital component of an internship experience when he reflected on his relationship with Mr. Jones, his WISE mentor. He said he had a "very special bond" with his mentor, who was "very willing to work with me." James also recalled Mr. Jones's reaction when he informed his mentor that he wanted to do an internship that entailed "going into the trenches to work on gay rights." James said that at first "I think he was shocked," but his mentor "rolled with the punches and agreed to help me. . . . I learned a lot due to his help."

All three of the individuals who participated in the Junior Firefighter Corps remembered their internship as a wonderful experience and an opportunity that many of their peers did not have. As previously mentioned, the opportunity for these young adults to join the volunteer fire department family and to be a part of such an invaluable public service was viewed as quite unique by each of the respondents. Peter said, "You always hear about the brotherhood or whatever, but you're going out and really putting your life on the line a lot and I would trust everyone in that firehouse. I had a couple of experiences when things went wrong, I fell through the floor and one of my friends, another kid my age, grabbed me before I went all the way through. I would go anywhere with them. I trust them like my brothers." Peter's recollection of this specific incident is only one example of how his internship experience was unique. Harry had similar feelings regarding his internship as a volunteer firefighter. Harry enrolled in the Junior Firefighter Corps immediately following the tragic events of September 11, 2001, and he recalled that "the program was supposed to start in September, but due to those events it was pushed back to October. . . . At that time everybody wanted to help, everybody wanted to know how to help out in traumas and stuff." The tragic events of 9/11 clearly sparked Harry's childhood dream of becoming a firefighter.

Tony, a childhood friend of Harry's, felt the same way about the Junior Firefighter Corps: "I remembered thinking over the summer it would be really cool to join the firefighters, I was like 12 or 13, but I never really thought I would. . . . Around here when something happens we're all there for each other. . . . That is why as such a young kid I looked up to everybody, no matter who they were it really taught me a lot." All of the conversations held with the junior firefighters echoed the same message: it was a powerful, memorable, and unique experience.

The adult-student relationships that the junior firefighters described were remarkable and made the experience quite unique for the research participants. The nature of the internship program itself encourages the development of this type of relationship. Given that these adolescents already feel a strong sense of commitment to their communities, the opportunity to develop what was called a "brotherhood" or "fraternity" naturally evolved. When Tony was asked about his relationship with Dan, the fire chief, he stated, "I like to describe it as close, but basically he is there when you need him. I remember having problems and I would call him up and talk with him. He's like a brother, he's very close." The importance of the relationship with his mentor was also revealed by Harry, who remembered the first phone conversation with Dan: "I was just sitting at home on my computer. . . . When I got off . . . All of a sudden my phone rang. . . . My buddy, Dan said, Jes, I can never get a hold of you. . . . We spoke a while ago and I told you that if you want to volunteer at the fire house it finally came through. . . . Why don't you stop down next week!" Harry provided deeper insight into his relationship when he explained that Dan is a "good family friend" whom he has known for many years and who used to take Harry and his friends down to the firehouse.

Peter recounted the first night he went to the firehouse when he "met up with Brian Jones, who was the captain at the time, and he said, 'How are you doing.' I knew him casually and he got me my gear and stuff. . . . I was put on the back of the truck with six people I didn't know. . . . They were all nice." It is clear through these interviews that the level of acceptance to the fraternity of volunteer firefighters is a powerful part of the experience for these high school students, an essential characteristic of community service programs, and marks an important departure from the adolescent society these students live within in high school.

The three respondents who participated in their high school science research program also remember the experience as special and unique. The science research program was quite different from the other two programs involved in this study in the area of academic rigor. The respondents talked about countless hours of background research just to learn about the subject area in which they chose to work for several years.

Rhami said that "it was such an ambiguous undertaking; you were off researching something you never heard of. . . . Simply just trying to struggle and find out what you should know and get the guidance that you need from your mentor and hope that your experiment works out well." He also reported that "from an academic rigor standpoint," the research program required him to get "well read on the topic, reading journals and internalizing some of that knowledge so I could actually ask the right question during research." As the valedictorian of his high school, it is noteworthy that he found the internship experience to be so intellectually challenging. For Rhami, high school was not very challenging, but the memories of his internship were quite different.

Debbie recalled similar feelings about the special opportunity she experienced through the internship program, and she also talked of feeling a passion for her pursuit and her commitment to making positive social change: "I like being aware of the change that I affect, to produce some triple cocktail that a person with HIV is now going to be able to take and decrease the chance of virus mutation and increase their life expectancy. It was amazing to see that I was a piece of that and I contributed to that." Debbie also remembered the unique relationship that she developed with the teacher in charge of the science research program. She said she "saw him more as a friend than teacher," and that relationship with her mentor provided a "certain honest aspect that you wouldn't necessarily get with a teacher where you have to watch what you say." Debbie reported many aspects of her internship experience that set the experience apart from her traditional schooling.

William also had distinct memories of the science research program and he recalled, "It was overall a really positive experience for me. . . . My research project was about the breeding habits of two species of mosquitoes that carried the West Nile virus." He said there was "a lot of media" about the issue, and it was "pretty important" and "not something you look into every day." William clearly had positive memories of his internship experience. He also vividly remembered the relationship he forged with his mentor. William said his mentor was "kind of wary given the fact that I was joining late," but the mentor was nonetheless "enthusiastic to help me out and very concerned that I catch up with the others." William also recalled that his mentor was "very supportive, very helpful, especially around the time of the competition," and was very "enthusiastic" in his support for William's work. The relationship obviously had a lasting impression on William, who was able to recall vivid details about it nearly four years later.

7

THE PORTAL TO SUCCESS AND PERSONAL GROWTH

As these college students reflected back on their internship experience, they identified certain qualities that were fostered through their high school internship. In this chapter, the students discuss how the formative experience of an internship helped them prepare for successful college careers. Faced with different challenges in postsecondary education, these students reported that their internship experiences enhanced their work ethic, provided them with the skills to develop productive relationships with their professors, and helped them find direction and clarity about career paths. The individuals provide powerful reflections about experiences that they felt set them apart from their peers in college and gave them essential tools they needed to succeed.

WORK ETHIC

Regardless of which internship program the students pursued, they said they felt that the learning experience helped them develop a heightened sense of commitment and challenged their work ethic. All of the respondents were challenged academically during their first year of college. They related their ability to be successful in college to the commitment and work ethic that was fostered during their internship experience in high school. A majority of the respondents reported that the internship was more challenging than their regular schoolwork and said that being confronted with these challenges during high school prepared them for the academic demands they faced in college. The responses from the students were passionate, personal, and authentic. They cited personal challenges they confronted and overcame because of the preparation they received in high school through their internship experience.

Debbie, who participated in the Science Research Program, stated: "I remember having to do a lot of work. That was probably the most applied I have ever been throughout my high school career." As she reflected on one of her regional competitions, she remembered that "in order to be competitive the amount of work that you do and what you present have a direct correlation. You know the quality of your presentation is going to be much higher the more time you put into it, and I made it to ISEF." Later in the interview, Debbie provided genuine reflections regarding the high standards she imposed on herself during the internship and her level of commitment to the individuals who were responsible for guiding her through this challenging endeavor. She said she believes that performance in the workplace "is a personal reflection of who you are," and she observed that "when your work directly reflects who you are, you want to make the best impression, you want the person who took you on to be proud that they took you on and you want the person that helped get you there to be proud that they got you there."

The common thread of personal commitment and excitement ran through each and every case study in this research project. James, who participated in an internship to promote an understanding of gay and lesbian rights, reported:

I did work harder at times because that was something that I really had a passion for. . . . The opportunity to do something that I really wanted to do fueled my work ethic. . . . I jumped right in. I was thrilled. If I could have I would have done it sooner. . . . Because I believed in it so much. . . . Because I'm gay and I had experiences in high school that I really didn't want any other high schooler to have to live through. When you're doing something you like and you know that it is going to be for a good, I was doing good work. It wasn't just for me, it was good work for the community, so of course that made me work harder and it was a lot more fun too.

The sense of community and work ethic was also a common theme throughout the responses from the individuals who participated in the Junior Firefighter Corps, as evidenced in the reflections by Harry, who said he "just developed a real strong work ethic, just like setting deadlines for myself and everything." He said the challenge "made me work harder and take more, I'm trying to think of the word, initiative, to get everything done before deadlines came about." Like James, Harry also spoke of an invaluable aspect of the experience when he stated, "I wasn't thinking as if I was doing this for school, I want to do it to better myself and better the community with helping and serving people." When Harry was asked how his internship impacted his success in college, he stated, "I always get my research papers done a couple of days in advance. . . . Just to get it done and out of the way. . . . Time management is the key. . . . It's not high school anymore." In part, he was able to overcome the challenges of college by relying on the preparation and experience he received through his high school internship.

The respondents also saw a difference between their level of commitment to their regular schoolwork in high school and the amount of time and work they committed to the internship experience. William recalled that "compared to high school course work I definitely worked a lot harder on my research. It wasn't like the standard regimented regents course, I had to think up my own curriculum, and come up with my own solutions." He recognized that he had to "work a lot harder," and in retrospect he acknowledged that "my work ethic for my research was greater than in my regular classes."

Rhami, who was the top student in his senior class, reported that "high school for me had always been more of a breeze." Yet he recalled certain highlights of his science research project quite differently:

> It wasn't necessarily the academic rigor of the program that was most challenging, it was such an ambiguous undertaking, you were off researching something that you've never heard of, that the science research person is telling you about, and you're simply just trying to struggle and find out what you should know and get the guidance that you need from your mentor and hope your experiment works out well. That aspect of it was challenging. . . . But from an academic rigor standpoint just getting well read on the topic, reading journals, and internalizing some of that knowledge so that I could actually ask the right question during research. . . . From my personal standpoint, I learned exactly what drives me and how I can succeed.

By his own admission, there were parts of the science research internship that required Rhami to work extremely hard and make a major commitment to his science research program. The validation of the academic rigor of internship programs is a concern for educators. In this context, it is important to note that the valedictorian of a high school admitted that his experiential learning project was a "struggle" while his traditional high school coursework was "a breeze."

Debbie echoed the same sentiment when she stated, "I believe that a lot of classes were absolutely pointless in high school, because of future application, I have none. But in this situation [science research] I am taking on something because I'm interested in it. . . . There's no such thing as getting an A or an A+ in your research. . . . It's something you really have to research. . . . It's the pursuit of knowledge."

Tanya, the recent immigrant from Haiti who participated in the WISE Program during her senior year in high school, made some intriguing comments regarding her high school education and her internship experience. She reported that when contrasted with high school in Haiti, "high school here was actually easy, I don't think the workload was tough in high school." By contrast, she found college "definitely hard," and she said that "my internship helped me with the know how, when the papers are due and I have a lot of work to do, I do it day by day." She said she believes her WISE internship "definitely showed me that I should never be a procrastinator." Given that she was in this country for only two years before attending college, it is clear the internship experience offered Tanya some invaluable insights and helped her establish essential academic practices in a very short period of time.

The themes of commitment and work ethic run through each respondent's story. Regardless of the student's academic ability, the nature of the internship experience, or which postsecondary institution the student attended, the internship experience had a memorable impact. The reflection of Peter, who always had to put in extra effort due to a learning disability, summarized his work ethic and commitment to a challenge when he genuinely stated:

> I've really got to buckle down and do this. I'm definitely struggling with some classes, but I know I am doing the best I can. . . . Overall I'm pretty successful. . . . I just sit back and say, hey, I got through everything else, I've gotten through a lot. This can't be any harder than that, and I really think about it, I look back and say everything I've come through, I can get through this. . . . This week will be better.

Peter's work ethic and commitment, coupled with his personal growth, have given him the necessary tools to be successful in postsecondary education.

ADULT RELATIONSHIPS

All of the respondents felt that their internship experience in high school fostered their ability to establish the adult relationships that are an expected part of postsecondary education. Their experiences enhanced their ability to communicate with their professors, adults, and new acquaintances in college. All of the individuals in the study also felt that they matured due to their internship experience, which at times set them apart from their peers in college. This natural transition to the adult world is one of the underlying components of the college experience that subsequently impacts the individual's success in the real world. As they faced certain challenges in college, they grew to recognize that their internships had taught them how to build adult relationships with others.

As Rhami reflected back to his college days, he credited his high school internship experience with "enhancing his people skills, especially when dealing with adults." He said that through the experience, "I learned how to work with people in a work environment," and he had the opportunity to get to know many of the researchers he worked with "as real people." The development of these relationships, he said, "made the experience much more real and more tangible for me." Debbie recalled the memorable relationship that she developed with her science research teacher because "they treat you like a peer. . . . They treat you like the person you want to be treated as, a friend."

Many of the respondents indicated that the significant adult relationships that they developed during their high school internship experiences provided them with a foundation to foster positive relationships with professors and other young adults in college. Tony discussed the challenges he faced in college regarding being away from home and participating in college athletics and recalled the importance of speaking to his mentor about those challenges:

Well, when I first went to Nichols I was happy to be there. I remember walking down the block talking to Dan, my chief now, who has basically been the person we all look up to because he started the Junior Corps unit. I was talking to him and said, "I don't like this, I don't really want to be away at home, what's the big deal." He explained his experiences when he went away to college. He thought it was awesome living on his own. The hard things I went through along with being away from home was trying out for the hockey team up there and the way it is at that school and many Division III, Division II and Division I schools. Freshmen who are trying out are usually 21 years old. . . . I'm a goalie and there were seven other goalies trying out, one was a returnee, one was a transfer from another school, so those two basically got it and one was a recruit. So, that made it very uncomfortable too, knowing that I couldn't do what I wanted to do, and that was one of the reasons I went to that school.

Many students dream of continuing their athletic careers in college and face similar challenges when those dreams are not fulfilled. Tony relied on the support of the mature adult relationship that he developed with his mentor in high school when faced with these challenges in college. The counsel that Dan provided allowed Tony to make an informed decision and transfer to a college closer to home, where he is currently having a positive postsecondary experience. When asked if the internship enhanced his ability to talk with adults, Tony said, "definitely, because I was so used to talking to older, mature people and showing them respect and what not, especially being around the chiefs, officers, and lieutenants. . . . When talking to professors I think they were a little more impressed."

James recalled the increased exposure to adults that he experienced through his internship. He said that through the internship experience, "I was speaking to adults all the time, as opposed to other high school students. . . . I think you need life experience to attain that level of communication." James saw his transition to college as seamless and reported that he was able to foster positive relationships with adults, starting with the relationship he developed with his mentor in high school. He said his relationship with Betty, the head of the advocacy program, was "a very special bond" and recalled, "we had a lot of time to put together programs and talked about what worked and what wouldn't work for different organizations. . . . So we got very close."

Harry echoed similar feelings about the adult relationships he developed during his internship. He said that what began as "a student-teacher relationship" grew into an "adult–young adult" relationship. Since then, he said, "as you grow older everything changes and the bonding and camaraderie changes. . . . I've bonded with more people from the fire department." Harry reflects back on his internship with fond memories of his personal growth in his ability to establish fulfilling relationships with adults.

Ann relied heavily on the adult relationships she developed outside of her immediate family, partially due to the fact that her parents were divorced. Her relationship with her mentor was unique, and she recalled, "he became a steady figure in my life who had many, if not all, of the answers to my questions, and when he didn't know the answers he would ask the right questions encouraging me to develop my own answers." She said she believes that in this relationship, "there was definitely a sense of inquiry and exchange of ideas based on mutual respect that occurred between myself and my mentor that did not exist at home." Ann credited her internship experience with giving her the confidence to approach professors and build positive relationships:

> When I got to college, not having the support group there, while I was doing very similar things because obviously you have a lot of presentations to do in college, because you even have to do even just simple stuff like I have to call my professor and make an appointment, because I'm having a problem with this paper and how do I do that. Because a lot of times you are in a class that's huge and the professor doesn't know your name, you know it was a little harder to do, obviously, without the support group of my teachers

from high school, but I also had a nice sort of security of knowing that well, I am allowed to do this, this is what I'm supposed to be doing now, it's not like I'm doing something that's forbidden to me. I'm allowed to call my professors and ask them for help. . . . I'm allowed to, you know, can you look over this paper before I hand it in, you know, for the final grade, and that sort of a permission that you give yourself that sometimes it could take a lot longer to give yourself that permission to actually interact with the real world once you're in college. But because I had already had a taste of it in high school, I remembered the experience and I can just say, "Well, I was actually successful in it in high school and I was only in twelfth grade." So now I'm a freshman in college, in a really good college, there's no reason why I can't handle this. So, that was nice.

Ann clearly stated that she felt prepared to handle the adult relationships she needed to establish in college as a result of the experience she gained through her high school WISE internship.

All of the respondents said they felt that their internship experience made them more mature and worldly. William remains a strong advocate for internship programs and said he believed, "It would definitely give them a better idea of what is expected of them as an adult as they mature into adults. I think on many fronts, it was a huge stepping stone for me, I mean it helped me to develop better as a person, just dealing with people every day." Harry was candid when he stated:

> Your whole public view changes and you realize when you're an adult you can't screw around. Like some high school kids horse around and want to do whatever, and then on Monday morning you see their names in papers, they get arrested for doing something. You can't do that anymore. . . . You're an adult now and you have to step up to the plate, it's the real world, you can't screw up anymore. . . . Yeah, it made me more of an adult person in college. . . . Because in college you're considered an adult and you have to make adult decisions.

Tony participated in the same internship program and said he believes that due to the heightened sense of maturity and responsibility he developed during his internship experience he was better equipped to help out a friend during an emergency situation: "My friend had to be taken to the hospital because of excessive drinking. . . . I knew what I had to do. . . . I was the one who looked after her, I was the one who took her to the hospital. I became a much more caring person. . . . This is the right thing to do." Tony said that when he assumed the responsibility to look after a friend, his peers commented, "I can't believe Tony is doing this."

Debbie credited her internship with enhancing her ability to communicate and network in the adult world because "it definitely forced me to be outspoken, I had no choice." She said that because of the challenge of her internship, "I really had to force myself out of the shell" and "I grew personal relationships. . . . It was an amazing experience to grow, to learn, and network." She also said she believes that those networking and interpersonal skills become "one of the most important things in your life. . . . It's who you know." Debbie clearly benefited from her internship experience, contributing to her maturity and self-confidence.

Peter said he felt that his experience as a junior firefighter contributed to his maturity and enhanced his ability to communicate with his professors in college. Peter said he is "more mature because of it. I think I'm better suited to discuss issues with my professor. There are a lot of kids who say, 'Hey, he did this to me.' Whereas I say, 'Well I didn't do this right, or whatever.' I think I'm able to better relate to the professor and talk to him, go to him and have a mature conversation." As previously stated, all of the respondents said they felt the experience made them more mature and provided them with a foundation to develop mature, effective adult relationships.

COLLEGE SUCCESS

All college students face certain unexpected demands in their first year of college. These challenges come in the form of academic, social, and emotional hurdles, many of which contribute to student failure in college. Each of the respondents clearly remembered certain obstacles they needed to overcome during their initial year in college. This research indicates that several of the important themes that emerged from the data—independence, achievement, passion, work ethic, and being able to build positive adult relationships—are qualities that provide an individual with a strong foundation for success in postsecondary education.

All of the respondents attributed their success in college in part to their internship experience in high school and said the internship program helped them cope with the academic demands of postsecondary education. James said he learned important skills that helped him in college:

> Participating in the internship during high school gave me a sense of responsibility in terms of creating, starting, and finishing projects. This helped me academically when I went to college because in college you are not monitored the way you are in high school. In college your projects are pretty much done on your own with no coaxing from teachers or parents.

Tony participated in the Junior Firefighter Corps, and he echoed the same sentiment as James when he recalled, "I realized what deadlines were and the responsibility I had in completing a given assignment. I also didn't want my teachers or my peers to think I was incapable of completing assignments." Tony and James refer to the notion of responsibility and completing work in a timely fashion as important aspects of academic success in college. William expanded on this important aspect of responsibility and independence and its influence on success in college when he stated, "Learning to work on your own I think was the most important thing. . . . There was a lot of free range and you had to do the work on your own." He said that through his experiential learning opportunity, "I learned to do my own work and motivate myself to do the work. . . . I think high school kids don't realize what that entails. . . . It's all your own doing. . . . No one is there to hold your hand every step of the way."

Several of the participants confirmed the importance of working in a different environment or on a project with some form of support and guidance from either a mentor or a teacher. Their testimony confirms the wisdom of John Dewey's educational philosophy when he spoke of the importance of the "genuine situation of experience"[1] and suggested that in a progressive society, it is essential that education permit more individualism so that a student is educated to "change . . . [a] freed individual, one who practically determines his own career."[2] It is clear in the words of these students that experiential learning supported their transition to college and adulthood. These sentiments were voiced by several of the respondents, including Ann:

> Participating in WISE gave me a forum in which I was simultaneously supported by my mentors and teachers, and put out there in the real world and told to make decisions on my own. This unique situation helped me so much because it allowed me to make mistakes, so to speak, this first time around, since the mistakes would not directly affect the rest of my life in the big ways that those same decisions would in college or beyond. I honestly think this is the biggest way in which WISE contributed to my academic success in college because I entered college already knowing what a job interview was, what a major presentation in front of important people was, and what it meant to have to be somewhere on time or else I would be in danger of being penalized in some way, like by being fired or even just reprimanded. This experience was invaluable to me in college, and still is.

A recent graduate of a prestigious university, Ann still attributes her academic success in part to her internship experience back in high school. Peter, a sophomore in college, responded in a similar manner to the same question. He said his internship "helped me a lot with just interacting with people and really knowing that going into a situation where I really didn't have a firm idea of what I was doing, I think firefighting helped me with facing challenges. . . . I was pretty strong with who I was when I went to college." Both Ann and Peter clearly believe that their internship experiences contributed to their personal confidence in facing challenges.

All of the respondents commented on the challenges that they faced during their first year of college. Time management was mentioned by several of the respondents, and their reflections regarding their internship experience clearly support the notion that their experience in high school helped them in their transition to college. Harry recounted that his internship "was kind of challenging at first because when I went to take my class I was playing sports and everything so I was trying to balance everything. . . . As soon as practice was over I got on the bus and went to the firehouse because I had made a commitment to both, so it was kind of challenging. Sometimes I had to leave class early so it worked out. I just had to manage school, social time, sports, and the firehouse." Later in the interview Harry reflected upon the workload in college and recalled "the whole adjustment to work and everything." He said it was clear to him that "it's not high school anymore. . . . They could really care less. . . . I knew it was going to be more and that was one of the challenges that I overcame." Harry credited his internship program with providing him with the attributes necessary to succeed in college because it "made me somewhat more of an adult person in college. In college you're considered an adult and you had to make adult decisions about work. It helped me with time management and helped me prioritize my tasks."

All of the respondents were surprised by the level of academic rigor in postsecondary education. Even Rhami, the valedictorian of his high school, noted the challenges of his first year of college. He said that while high school for him "had always been more of a breeze," the first year of college "was a nightmare, the first semester was a rude awakening, so I worked harder and it became a breeze again." Rhami said his exposure to his real-world experience provided him with the tools he would need in college because it "made me more committed and it also reinforced my already very strong work ethic."

Debbie recalled that when she first went to college, "I was not accustomed to the workload. Everyone in my engineering class had the same SAT scores, the same honors classes and high GPAs. They all had a similar background and that was hard to swallow." She said that to compete among her peers, "I had to work a lot harder. . . . You had to live on your own and fend for yourself." When asked how her internship prepared her for future challenges, she said, "I remember having a lot of work. That was probably the most I have ever applied myself throughout my high school career." She said her internship "was demanding, especially to be competitive, which is what I try and strive to be. . . . I always strive to be competitive and that's one of the things I learned. . . . I really had to put my all into it and I really had to focus." Debbie clearly believed that her internship strengthened her ability to face such challenges and thus contributed to her successful transition to college. Peter expressed the same sentiment when he said, "I just kind of think back and say, hey, I got through everything else, I've gotten through a lot, this can't be any harder than that, I look back and say, 'You know, everything I've come through, I can get through this. This week will be better.'" Peter's internship provided him with a strong foundation to face the academic challenges of postsecondary education. William also recounted how the science research program prepared him for the academic challenges because it was "very different. I mean nobody else ever did anything like this in high school. I think it prepared me for the kind of work that I would be doing in college, the more independent work, research skills in terms of projects and presentations. . . . The regent's classes in high school didn't stress that very much."

Research on college attrition reinforces the fact that the student's ability to face the academic rigor of postsecondary education is not the only hurdle one must clear to be successful in college.

The student's social adjustment to college is extremely important, and if it is not managed correctly it can result in academic failure. Rhami attested to the importance of his high school internship in this regard when he reported that "socially it [college] was also an eye opener, and I think that part of the experiences that I had during the research course actually helped me transition out in the world on my own." Tanya echoed this sentiment when she said her experience helped her not only learn more about herself and society, but also about what life would be like beyond college in the field of psychology:

> Oh, it definitely opened my eyes and broadened my horizon because working with these physically handicapped children, which was something I was never exposed to before, furthered my knowledge and my understanding about life. You understand that you can't take some things for granted. . . . It definitely made me more mature and now that I am in college I'm learning more about exactly how to deal with society and how to deal with children with certain disorders, it definitely gave me a better understanding of what it's really like to work in the field of psychology. It definitely helped me adjust to college life.

James was quite surprised when he entered college. He commented on his experience regarding social freedom and his social adjustment. James said, "I did what I did in high school, which was basically find a group of friends that shared common interests and common philosophies. . . . It was fantastic to be more independent and to be able to do more for myself so I had a great social adjustment to college." James credited his internship experience with helping him develop a better ability to communicate with people because during that experience "I was at a level where I was speaking to adults all the time. . . . I learned how to express myself. . . . I don't believe that is something you can completely learn in high school. I think you need life experience to attain that level of communication." James stressed that the ability to effectively communicate contributes to the individual's successful social adjustment in college.

CAREER PLANNING—SORTING

Several of the respondents felt that their internship experience supported them in determining certain career paths upon graduation from college. The undergraduate years in college can be challenging for students who are unclear about what vocation they want to pursue. Many students find it difficult to declare a major early in their undergraduate studies and spend their first two years taking liberal arts courses while they sift through their career options. Several of the participants in this study spoke about this challenge. They felt, however, that the internship experience in high school sharpened their focus regarding future career options.

Five of the nine participants in the study said they believed the internship provided them with a snapshot of a career they were interested in pursuing. Tanya viewed the internship experience as a portal to her future career. She said she "wanted to end my high school experience differently. I didn't want to take regular English for the sake of it. And WISE was a way for me to explore everything, and I had a chance of working in a field that I was interested in, which was psychology." Later in the interview she said she had stayed on the same career path since her internship experience and reported, "Yes, I am definitely pursuing it. I only have three classes left in my major. I took most of my psychology classes already, and I am doing a concentration in developmental psychology of disabled children." Tanya's internship experience not only guided her toward the field of study in which she was interested, but also exposed her to the population of children that she wanted to work with as a professional in that field.

Peter, a junior firefighter whose father is an attorney in the town where he grew up, offered an interesting reflection of the impact of his internship on his career plans:

> I got into firefighting, and it's a volunteer organization that I kind of looked at it as I'll go and do this and then I'll be a lawyer in town and still join the volunteer firefighters wherever I was. I think once I really started getting in there, I really fell in love with it. I really fell in love with the job and I really want that to be part of my life. I really just want to work on that for the rest of my life. I think slowly and surely as I got deeper and more involved in the firefighting and saw what was going on, I think probably the first time I went to a real fire, and went inside, I think I came outside and said this is really what I want to do, it kind of shaped what I've done, I'm trying to get into shape now. . . . I'm studying for fire exams, the New York fire exam is in a couple of months, it's in October.

Quite frequently, high school students pursue the careers of their fathers or mothers, and Peter believed that he would travel the same path as his father. The internship experience, however, helped Peter find his own calling when he was exposed to a career in which he discovered a passion for the work. Later in the interview when Peter was asked where he would like to be in five years, he said, "Well, hopefully I'll be a New York City firefighter and hopefully I'll still be doing theater and still involved in the volunteer fire department. That's where I see myself." Peter's interests in professional firefighting and in the technical side of theater are currently his professional pursuits.

Tony's response was also quite interesting when he spoke of his career goals. The strength of the family and community bonds that he established growing up in his hometown was evident:

> Well, I still have my father's company, me and my brother are planning on taking over, but since being in the fire department, I've been looking at fire tests, more leaning towards the police test. . . .

I'm a finance major in college, my father owns a pretty successful company, and he's been open for twenty-seven years.

When asked whether his ultimate goal would be to become a civil servant police officer or firefighter and then to run his father's business, he said he was exploring ways to pursue both:

> Yeah, it depends on what department you work for. You can work three days a week with some departments, so between me and my brother, yeah, I would say we can run it.

Both Tony and Peter have a dream of careers in public safety, either in firefighting or police work. The third junior firefighter, Harry, said he also would love to be a professional firefighter, but he said he recognized that it may not be a realistic goal:

> I mean I'd love to be a fire fighter. I've taken some of the tests and agility, just to see where I would end up on the list. But pretty much the resident thing for each city is a big factor. They frown upon non-residents getting it over residents. . . . Of course it opened up career goals. I mean, I'm going to school majoring in sports marketing, sports management, yeah, it definitely opened up other things. You got to see the whole picture of professional firefighting. You got to see the job opportunities and all the different goals you want to reach. Many people know the city of Yonkers has some of the highest paid firefighters in the nation. Everyone would love to get on there just to get paid and everything, but you realize you have to see where you get to start and what you want to make out of your life.

While Harry may still hold remnants of his childhood dream of becoming a firefighter, he has had the opportunity to make a clear assessment of how that pursuit matches up against other career goals.

Ann participated in the WISE Internship Program in high school and worked in the theater district for the last semester of her senior year in high school. She said her internship experience reinforced her confidence and awareness of her creative abilities.

She said that through the WISE Program, "one other personal attribute that was strengthened was belief in my creativity. . . . My creative growth as a result of both my successes and failures was huge. . . . I decided to write a short play as part of my project." Ann's passion for writing, which was a major part of her internship experience, was instrumental in helping her refocus her career plans:

> I am studying to become children's/teen librarian. Another goal I have is to get published in one of many areas—scholarly essay, children's book, and memoir being the three that I am most passionate about. WISE actually had a direct impact on these new goals as well, because in terms of writing it got me to produce more writing than I ever have. . . . WISE actually showed me that I *could* write on a regular basis, that I have the ability to do this thing I love so much. As for my decision to become a kids' librarian, WISE actually contributed to that as well, since the main reason I want to work with kids is to help foster the natural sense of curiosity and questioning that every child has the right to experience, and my memories of WISE are proof that this is something that helps a person to grow into someone more ready and able to contribute to society and the quality of life.

Their words are powerful because in retrospect, their internships were such formative experiences in their lives and gave them critical skills that continued to guide them as they prepared to transition from college to adulthood.

NOTES

1. J. Dewey, *Democracy and Education* (New York: The Free Press, 1944), 163.

2. J. Dewey, *Lectures in the Philosophy of Education, 1899* (New York: Random House, 1966), 35.

8

THE IMPACT OF THE INTERNSHIP EXPERIENCE ON LIFE BEYOND COLLEGE

Upon completion of the undergraduate experience, many college graduates lack direction regarding career plans or options. The stories told in this book highlight the contributions the internship experience made when students later navigated decisions about future plans. The internship experience provided these young adults with real-life experiences that allowed them to make informed choices regarding career options. All of the individuals in this text had established career goals and clear ideas about their future pursuits, helping them make a seamless transition to life after their sixteen years of formal education.

Each respondent also said their internship experience contributed to their personal growth. Several cited common areas of personal growth, which have been already addressed as one of the emergent themes. It became apparent, however, that there were several other areas in which respondents experienced personal growth, and they are as unique as the internship experiences themselves. Those insights are discussed in this chapter.

PERSONAL GROWTH

Rhami said he felt that the experience improved his "leadership capabilities" and enhanced his drive towards "professional achievement." Rhami said that through his internship experience, "I learned exactly what drives me and how I can succeed." He also said that the experience improved his ability "to talk with people. . . . I was very shy."

As part of her WISE Internship, Ann said she was provided an opportunity to explore her creative ability through the experience of writing a short story. She recounted:

> The biggest way in which WISE affected my values and beliefs was in validating for me that creative pursuits are just as valuable and have just as much worth as other kinds of pursuits. Creating and making the time to do what you love is important and necessary—I realized this when I decided I would write a short play as part of my project, rather than simply going to a theater-related internship once or twice a week. This is a belief I hold to this day, and without WISE to really give it real-world validity, I am not sure I would have continued to feel this way about the act of creating past the insulated world of high school.

Ann elaborated on the lasting impact of her internship:

> I'd say my sense of self-confidence and worth was definitely strengthened during WISE—it has to be when I am being treated like an adult, like someone who is capable of contributing something of value, and for this I am very grateful. My ability to articulate myself also improved, which makes sense because I had to speak with leaders in my field on a regular basis, and then present my findings in a forty-minute presentation at the end of the program. One other personal attribute that was strengthened through WISE was belief in my creativity. WISE gave me a forum in which I could try out new things that may or may not be successful creatively, but my creative growth as a result of both the successes and the failures was huge.

Tony said he became more self-assured: "It made me more confident with myself. . . . I was no longer afraid to meet new people. . . . I became more of an outspoken individual." He said the internship also "strengthened my values, it made me realize what type of person I was and it made me value friendship and family." Tony's sense of trust and family was enhanced by his internship experience. Although he experienced a difficult transition the first year of college, he credited his internship experience with "helping him adjust to learning environments. . . . It helped me adjust a lot more to the college scene."

Tanya revealed growth in other areas when she said her internship helped her to become "more patient. . . . I'm definitely more accepting of all kinds of people now. . . . I'm more understanding, I have more empathy. . . . I feel their pain. . . . I grew up, it opened my eyes." These are powerful comments, and important insights in the journey from adolescence to adulthood. Tanya said her experience working with disabled children made her "a better person. . . . It was hard to accept different kinds of people that I've never really come across in my life, but as I was getting to know them, as I had a chance to know them more and more, I fell in love with them. It was tough, but it was exciting, it was a great new adventure." Tanya's powerful recollections suggest her internship was truly transformative and an experience that will remain with her throughout her life.

When Peter reflected on his volunteer firefighter experience he acknowledged that "it changed me a lot. I definitely look at the world in a different way, it showed me the good side of the world and the bad side of the world. I think it has given me some leadership skills and a lot more confidence." He said his internship experience helped him discover more about himself and as a result, "I was pretty confident with who I was and when I went to college I kind of kept with that." Peter said that he has reached back and reflected on his internship when difficult situations arose in college, and it has helped remind him, "Hey, I got through everything else. I've gotten through a lot. This can't be any harder than that, I can get through this." Peter provided some additional reflection when he recalled, "I never really understood it until I joined. You always heard about the brotherhood, but you're going out putting your life on the line and I would trust everyone in that firehouse."

James's internship placed him in environments that were not welcoming as he traveled from school to school talking about gay and lesbian rights. As he reflected on some of the experiences, he summed it up quite well when he stated, "I gained a great deal of personal confidence. I learned how to present myself in a mature and commanding way." James also reported that his experience impacted his beliefs because it fueled his passion for political and social reforms and helped him understand the importance of "being part of a greater whole" and encouraging others to fight for civil liberties. James was fortunate to participate in an internship for which he possessed such passion.

Harry said that his internship experience was a profoundly important experience because "there is a lot of personal growth. I mean it just makes you a better person." Furthermore, he said, "You feel better about yourself when you help other people. And when people thank you. . . . It makes you feel better when people congratulate you in public." The nature of the community service internships clearly provides an opportunity for the enhancement of an individual's sense of self-worth through selfless, and even courageous, acts of service.

Harry said that when he attended college he knew many students "who were going to drop out, and they never come back. . . . They would party all weekend and then drop out." Harry reported that he took a very different approach to his college experience and sought challenges in postsecondary education. He said that he "took classes that would challenge myself. . . . You get a broader range of knowledge and everything, of different topics." It is obvious that Harry had a more mature, adult perspective toward college and his future than many of his freshman classmates, which he attributed to his internship experience. He said that it was through his internship experience that he realized, "You're an adult now, you have to step up to the plate, it's the real world. You can't screw up anymore."

William said his internship helped him develop the skills to work independently because "you really learn to work on your own and motivate myself to do the work." It is imperative for college students to possess self-motivation when they are on their own. William indicated that he learned how to accept responsibility like an adult because in the internship experience, "It's all you; it's all your own doing." William also identified some ways in which the internship led to important personal growth because "socially it was a huge stepping stone for me, I mean it helped me develop better as a person." This personal growth was accompanied by a better understanding of the real world because he learned "they [fellow researchers] are people just like you are. . . . You get a real appreciation for what they are trying to teach you and the type of person they are."

Debbie provided some interesting responses regarding the personal growth that she attributed to her internship experience. She said the internship forced her to "become outspoken, I had no choice, I really had to force myself out of the shell." Her internship experience provided her with the self-assurance and confidence to "speak with people and share her ideas with individuals in the research community." Debbie added that in retrospect, the internship was a powerful experience because "these are the formative years, you're very impressionable, and you're sensitive to ideas." She experienced personal growth, and she said her values "were changed."

These are the genuine and unique reflections of nine successful college students or recent college graduates. Their stories are from the heart, so listen to their words. All of the members of the academic community need to heed their advice. The next chapter will set forth certain recommendations based on their reflections.

9

RECOMMENDATIONS FOR PARENTS, SCHOOLS, STUDENTS, AND POSTSECONDARY INSTITUTIONS

There will be many recommendations made in this chapter. All of the adults involved in the life of an adolescent share in the responsibility for each student's success. Indeed, it does take a village to raise a child.[1] The roles of high school and college educators, parents, members of the community, relatives, and the students themselves are discussed in this chapter, highlighting the contributions by each group that are necessary to help the student make a successful passage to college and life beyond.

Internship opportunities for adolescents have been incorporated in many school districts while many other districts are investigating the possibility of including these programs as a curricular offering. This text investigated the inclusion of a variety of internship programs as a *formal* component of a student's educational program in high school. We have discussed the short- and long-term contributions that formal internship programs make to the student's individual growth during their secondary and postsecondary experience. Current literature indicates that internship and mentoring programs "make learning relevant in their lives by linking their schooling with 'real world' experience."[2]

Advocates for experiential learning opportunities cite many shortcomings of the current liberal education that we offer our children in public schools. But including internship and mentoring programs within the mainstream of public education "is a powerful pedagogical strategy that encourages students to make meaningful connections between content in the classroom and real life experiences."[3]

This chapter will examine the role of parents, schools, and students in fostering student involvement in internship experiences. Parents must be involved in their child's schooling from the beginning of high school in order to help counsel and support their child in the process of identifying and engaging in a rewarding internship experience. We will discuss the challenges that confront high schools in planning for effective and rigorous internship programs and incorporating those programs into the school so that students can balance their experiential learning with classes and other activities. Students must invest themselves in the process as well so they can plan for their internship, research options for experiential learning, and select the right internship program for them. Finally, the role of colleges is discussed, including the need to improve admission standards so they examine the overall experiences of the applicant and the need to provide meaningful transition support for incoming freshmen.

THE PARENTS' ROLE

Every parent sends their child off to high school believing that their child will grow and mature into a responsible adult while struggling with the challenges of adolescence. After reading the stories from this text, hopefully all parents will see the need to become involved in their child's education and to advocate for experiential learning experiences. Parents of an adolescent would embrace a program or experience that develops their child's independence, gives them a sense of accomplishment, helps them discover a passion, provides a unique experience, improves their work ethic, fosters adult relationships, lays the groundwork for their success in college, and helps them initiate career planning and sort through their future options. The reflections of the students in this text identified growth in all of these areas.

The promising news is that today, more than ever, parents have become active participants in their children's education. Parents need to be actively engaged in their child's education throughout high school. They must strike the delicate balance between becoming over-involved and allowing their child to have too much freedom during the most challenging years of their life. As a parent, you will be making valuable contributions to your child's transition to adulthood. Parents need to keep a watchful eye over their child's experiences. All adolescents need to develop a sense of autonomy and the ability to deal with challenging situations as they arise. Parents cannot send their child off to college *defenseless*, being unable to cope with the stress of postsecondary education during one of the most difficult transitions in their young life.

Although adolescents may constantly send messages to their parents to be left alone as they stumble through adolescence, it is a time in the child's life when *they need you more than ever*. As adults, however, we need to understand where we will fit into their life and *stand beside them but stay out of their way*. Parenting is not an easy charge, and many of us ask ourselves questions as to whether or not we are making correct decisions regarding our children. Parents need to be partners and a part of their child's life: involved in their schooling, community activities, relationships with their extended family and their child's peers.

The High School Years: Parents' Checklist

The high school years will be challenging for both you and your child. I have worked in public education for almost thirty years, and

I've seen that even the "model adolescents" prove to be challenging to their parents. As previously mentioned, your child will be developing at an extraordinary rate of speed and will eventually become a young adult, but don't let their size and evolving maturity fool you. They are still children.

There are no textbook answers for parents on how to manage their adolescent children. If there were, Dr. Phil would no longer be syndicated. There is no boilerplate solution for the challenges of adolescence. All parents, children, and family dynamics are unique. When we consider the adolescent's perspective on their ever-changing world, the challenges of these years are even more daunting.

Therefore, as a parent, you need to keep in mind the following basic tenets of effective parenting:

- Communicate with your child
- Listen to your child
- Find your place in your child's world
- Do not be selfish with your time
- Respect your child's opinion
- Stress the importance of family time
- Stress the importance of education
- Hold your child responsible
- Teach respect
- Allow your child to gain independence and autonomy
- *Love* your child

It is not the intention of this text to serve as a guide to parenting adolescents; however, these are vital aspects to being an effective parent and building a strong foundation and effective relationship with your developing child. They will seek your guidance and counsel when they trust you are there for them.

Stand Alongside Your Child but Stay Out of the Way

Student participation in an internship program is not a simple process. Schools need to structure the program and clearly articulate the expectations to all members of the academic community. Parents need to take an active part in their child's education.

Due to the developmental level of the adolescent and the need to provide them with opportunities to develop their individual autonomy, the adults in the child's life need to be careful to stand alongside their child but stay out of their way. This is not an easy charge. Parents need to start the process of promoting their child's autonomy prior to their high school years. Students in high school need to be able to be their own advocates and engage in adultlike behaviors. The apron strings need to be released. Children must learn to make decisions, some of which will be questionable, and be given the chance to learn and grow from the trials and tribulations of adolescence. As parents, however, it is of utmost importance that we keep our children safe while letting them grow.

No one knows your child better than you do. This is the main reason why you need to be involved in your child's education throughout high school. But as your child matures, you need to stand beside your young adult and articulate your concerns as they navigate adolescence. As partners in your child's education, you need to be there for support and guidance, not to micromanage your child's decisions. Because you do know your child best, communicating with school authorities regarding the internship process is important both to meeting your needs as a parent and to the success of the program.

The Internship Process

Throughout the internship experience, parents need to be intimately involved and embrace the importance of these experiences. Parents will receive guidelines from their child's school regarding the internship process along with timelines and ways in which they can help. Well-structured internships like the WISE Program, Science Research, and many community service programs clearly define the role of the parent throughout the internship process. As parents read this chapter they need to keep in mind the reflections of the students who participated in these programs. The students felt a sense of independence, faced academic rigor, enhanced their work ethic, had real-life work opportunities, built positive relationships with adults, and had a unique learning experience. All of these factors are what helped make the internships a portal to their personal success.

The parent's role in the internship process varies from district to district. Students have the opportunity to enroll in these programs at various times during their high school tenure. For example, students can enroll in Science Research Programs as early as their sophomore year of high school, whereas the WISE Program is a senior year alternative program. It is important for parents to fully understand the offerings in their schools.

One of the fundamental hurdles that internship programs will face in high schools is the reluctance of parents to accept a radical departure from traditional education. Parents are very comfortable knowing that their child is safe within the confines of their neighborhood high school, under the watchful eye of professional educators. As previously mentioned, however, in many cases, a teenager's immersion in the adolescent society that forms within schools can have detrimental effects. If you have experienced being a parent of a child during the senior year of high school, you can fully understand the need to promote activities that challenge students and promote their personal growth.

There is usually an orientation meeting to introduce and outline the internship program and answer any questions that parents may have. Understandably, parents who attend these meetings have concerns since internships are a departure from traditional schooling. School administrators, counselors, and teachers who are involved in the programs provide the parents with information regarding their unique programs. It is important to ask any questions you have and inquire into the success of the program and how the specific internships are established. Remember, the experience must be unique and close to your child's heart. Students are usually required to attend these orientation meetings with their parents to discuss the internship opportunities available. The student's role in the internship selection process is essential.

After your child has found an internship program that they want to pursue, parents need to acknowledge the efforts by their child's mentor. They can write a note to the mentor thanking them for the wonderful opportunity they are providing. Parents should stress the fact that they will be there if needed and invite the mentor to engage in an open dialogue regarding the child's progress. This is still another opportunity for the parent to stand alongside their child but stay out of the way.

Meet Your Child's Counselor in Ninth Grade

School counselors are very busy people. In many schools, high student caseloads make it impossible for them to provide your child with the guidance they need. It is of utmost importance that you meet with your child's counselor early in their high school career and get to know them. As high school counselors read this chapter, they may be quietly cringing at this recommendation. Although they are very busy people, they enjoy casual meetings, talking about your child and getting to know him or her the best they can. These meetings are refreshing to educators. Too often meetings with parents involve putting out fires or dealing with problems. These are the meetings that counselors dread!

This will give you an opportunity to have an open discussion with a trained professional and begin to forge a positive, supportive relationship. Throughout your child's tenure in high school you will be involved in their scheduling of courses, performance from year to year, and, eventually, postsecondary opportunities. It is also vital to talk with the counselor about the internship opportunities that are available to your child during their senior year of high school. You will need to be well versed on the internship opportunities offered by the school to facilitate a conversation with your child. Later in this chapter we will talk about an effective internship program and how schools may need to change the senior year experience to better meet the needs of your children as they prepare for life after high school.

Parents need to remember, however, that the internship opportunity must be dear to your child's heart in order for it to be successful. This is where your mature, grounded input will be vital, and you can help your son or daughter sift through a confusing world of options and benefit from a unique internship experience. Don't try to relive your life through your child's internship experience. It will most certainly fail, and your son or daughter will not benefit. It must be their experience. Stand alongside your child but do not get in the way.

Monitor Academic Rigor

Parents need to be concerned about the academic rigor of the internship experience. All students who participate in successful internship programs should be challenged academically. This question should be raised long before the internship program begins, placing a vital charge upon the secondary educators to ensure that academic rigor will be maintained. The WISE Program requires the maintenance of a detailed portfolio that includes extensive research on their senior project. The Science Research students are obviously challenged academically via hundreds of hours of research; the community service volunteers are required to take extensive coursework outside of high school. As a parent, you need to ensure that the experience does not include a watered-down curriculum. The child needs to benefit from the real-life experience in many ways, including challenging the student academically.

One of the main reasons student internship programs are being entertained by many districts is to combat the dreaded disease known as "senioritis." Internship programs require the students to leave the comfort of their adolescent society, go out into the real world, and be challenged in their new environment. The students interviewed for this text said that their departure from traditional education provided them with an experience that was critically important and gave them an opportunity to experience extensive personal growth that helped them successfully navigate the transition from high school to college.

Parental Involvement with the Internship Experience

Once you have established a working relationship with your child and the school, there are certain aspects of the transition to the senior year of high school that must be discussed. Parents' involvement regarding internship programs must increase during the fall semester of the junior year of high school because many internship programs are not available until the senior year of high school. The internship experience is a vital component of your child's secondary school experience and will give him or her exposure to the real world while living in the supportive setting of your home. There are several basic tenets that parents must keep in mind regarding the internship opportunities available to their child.

- Be informed about your child's options and ensure the academic rigor of those options.
- Have conversations regarding the benefits of their choice of internship experiences.
- Inquire whether this internship experience could help the child clarify career options.
- Determine whether the internship reflects your child's choice. Assess whether your child will be able to juggle their regular academics with the internship program.
- Assess how the program will fit into your child's extracurricular schedule.

By remembering these guiding questions you will be supporting your child as they prepare to enter a meaningful and personal internship experience.

THE ROLE OF THE SECONDARY SCHOOL

Successful internship programs are not developed in our high schools overnight. The establishment of such programs takes extensive planning, a fiscal commitment from the school, and the assignment or hiring of staff members who are willing to do the work to make the program a success. Due to the nature of internship programs and the fact that it is a detour from traditional education, a strategic planning process is essential to ensuring that the program is embraced by all members of the academic community. In order for the internship program to be successful, the task force must develop a program that fits the need of the school's academic community and the community at large. Therefore, there is no template for an effective program that can be applied to all high schools. This text will provide school officials and educators with suggestions and guidelines. They will need to apply their expertise, professional training, understanding of their school philosophy, and understanding of the needs of the community to develop an effective internship program that has broad support.

The Strategic Planning Process

In public education today, programs are introduced for various reasons. They may be designed to align educational reform with the powerful recent political movement to emphasize standards and increased assessment. They may be driven by educators who have been looking at their own unique educational community and made a determination of what is best for their children. The internship movement addresses both these camps. Advocates of internships seek to improve student performance and success along the K–16 continuum by improving the chance of success in college, as well as providing their students with powerful, authentic learning experiences.

Academic communities engage in the strategic planning process to address educational reform of this nature. All of the stakeholders of the school community participate in this process, including students, teachers, parents, administrators, and members of the community. The commitment of these various stakeholders in the process must be facilitated, nurtured, and cultivated by skilled administrators who are capable of providing this diverse group with direction, a sense of accomplishment, and personal ownership regarding the specific initiatives they are addressing.

Unlike other educational reform, the internship movement places additional challenges before a strategic planning task force. In order to provide the students with a viable internship experience, along with allowing them to participate in their school community and extracurricular activities, the implementation of such a program requires a drastic change in the educational philosophy of the district, educators, administrators, parents, and students.

Shift in Educational Philosophy

This will be the first, and most critical, hurdle that the strategic planning task force must clear. Straying from traditional education is troubling to many. Students leave the comfort of their schools and seek knowledge and learning experiences outside of the traditional classroom. The students will no longer be in contact every day with the teachers that were hired by the district and whom parents in the community have come to trust. It is inherent in human nature to have reservations about the unknown, and the initial questions regarding an internship program will revolve around this critical issue. This reinforces the importance of proper planning and a commitment by the strategic planning task force.

In order to address the concerns of individuals on the task force, its members need to visit various workplaces that have welcomed student internships in the past. The options are many, including local political offices, medical and science research facilities, hospitals and childcare facilities, elementary schools, and small, local businesses. Once these visits have been made and the members of the task force realize the unique nature of these programs, the individuals who have committed their time to participate in this initiative will develop an appreciation for the value of an internship experience.

All of the members of the task force are concerned about the educational opportunities provided for their students or they would not have made the commitment to participate in developing an internship initiative. Academic rigor and the monitoring of student progress will be a major concern of the task force. Questions will arise that need to be answered. The internship programs cited in this text challenged the students academically, while providing them with an authentic learning experience. The underlying tenet of this text is to prepare students to be successful in college by providing them with challenging yet unique learning experiences outside the walls of our high schools.

Academic Rigor and Relevance

Earlier in this text we spoke about the Rigor and Relevance model[4] and how it is applicable to the high school student internship experience. Daggett defined academic rigor as the passage through six stages, from a basic understanding of the information that we call knowledge to the ability of the individual to synthesize and evaluate that knowledge through the application to real-world situations.

This framework is supported and enhanced through an internship experience that maintains a certain level of academic rigor while making learning relevant. All of the internship experiences discussed in this text support Daggett's paradigm of Rigor and Relevance. You have been briefly introduced to Debbie, one of the science research students who participated in their project for several years. These students worked countless hours in the research facility over the summer between their junior and senior years of high school. Each participant felt that there was extensive academic rigor in their project. Rhami, the valedictorian of his high school, was constantly seeking information and knowledge to be able to make contributions to the field of research. Debbie worked endless hours researching possibilities to make the world a better place for victims of AIDS. William classified himself as an average student in high school who conducted countless hours of research investigating a serious public health issue, the West Nile virus.

The knowledge base required for these three students to conduct such extensive research indicates that their internships demanded a high level of academic rigor and their research studies were real and relevant. These students also were challenged in the area of public speaking because they had to make formal presentations to renowned research scientists. They spoke of the hours of preparation it took to develop dynamic presentations for local, regional, and national competitions, and they each felt that they made great strides in this area. The passion that these students had for their work was heard through their responses in chapters 5 and 6. This combination of academic rigor and relevance places the experience of these students in quadrant D of Daggett's framework.

The students who participated in the senior alternative program also were challenged with some forms of academic rigor but not at the same level as the science research students. The WISE Program requires students to maintain daily logs, and an exit project and presentation are required. The academic rigor, however, comes in different forms depending upon the nature of the internship. For example, James, whom you have met briefly, chose to advocate for the gay rights of high school students working for a nonprofit agency. He was a member of a team who visited public high schools to talk about issues of concern for gay students. He described several experiences that one could only imagine to be challenging, stressful, and quite demanding and tested his ability to speak publicly and persuasively on a somewhat controversial subject. His ability to speak passionately about the topic was supported by his background on the stage and in theater. The academic rigor of these public speaking experiences could be considered quite challenging. James demonstrated an ability to both understand and care deeply about the plight of these students and advocate on their behalf. These factors made the experience extremely relevant and place his experience in quadrant B of the framework and possibly quadrant D.

The community service internship participants were extremely passionate about their experience. In chapter 6 you met Peter, who told of a dangerous experience he encountered one night and how it reinforced his sense of brotherhood with the other firefighters. The students must also participate in coursework to achieve Firefighter 1 status, which is required of all volunteer firefighters. The rigor of the coursework would place the internship in the bottom half of the framework regarding academic rigor. It is obvious, however, that the students need to apply the knowledge that they learned in the coursework. In the area of relevance, the challenges of the program clearly place the experiences of these young firefighters in quadrant B. These individuals continue to be involved to date in the volunteer firefighter program and are pursuing lifelong dreams of becoming professional firefighters or police officers.

The application of this framework to these nine internship experiences is a starting point from which to look at the place of internship programs in our schools. These internship experiences placed students where they could be successful and maintain a balance acceptable to the individual between academic rigor and relevance. The personal nature of these nine experiences provides us with guidelines to implement successful internship experiences for our students.

Relationships

The students also described relationships they formed with adults that were quite different from the student-adult relationships that evolve in our high schools today. The unique nature of the experiences, coupled with the passion that these students felt for the work they did in their internships, facilitated the development of healthy and productive young adult–adult relationships.

Earlier we talked about the power of the adolescent culture and student world and how that phenomenon can have detrimental effects on the individual's development and transition to adulthood. The childhood and lifelong relationships that are fostered through years of public schooling begin to dissipate upon graduation from high school, leaving the student with little peer and emotional support as they confront one of the most challenging transitions of their short life. Is it any wonder then why so many of these students fail to make the transition successfully?

The reflections of the individuals presented in chapters 6 and 7 highlight the great value they placed on the adult relationships they established during their internship experiences. They were required to change social membership and learning environments. The high school internship experience allowed these students to make this difficult transition with the support of guidance professionals, family, and friends who were available to guide, counsel, and support them during their last year of formal secondary education. The benefits of these experiences clearly enhanced certain attributes of these young adults and provided important mortar for each of their bridges to college success and personal growth.

The design of the internship programs and their academic rigor will be a decision that must be made by the strategic task force. The internship programs in this text required extensive research in the chosen field of the internship, culminating in a research document, additional coursework, formal presentations, and the maintenance of a daily journal involving personal reflections and creative writing.

It is critical that the suggestions made by the educators on the task force represent the educational philosophy of their school. This is not an easy charge. The staff members, including the administrators, need to provide the entire professional staff with an opportunity to provide input regarding their expectations about the academic rigor of the internship program. Since many of the teachers and counselors in the school will serve as mentors for the students, they must have ownership of the initiative. This is especially challenging in larger high schools, where there is clearly a day-to-day disconnect between academic disciplines and departments. This is why a strategic planning task force must undertake this work over a long, yet defined, period of time.

Impact on Staffing and Scheduling

Educational initiatives have an impact on the staffing in our schools, whether it be providing students with additional instruction to meet their educational needs to perform better on standardized tests or introducing innovative educational programs. The impact of an internship program on staffing will depend upon the philosophy of the district and the commitment that the academic community is willing to make towards the internship initiative. The stories and findings discussed earlier in this text make the argument that the internship program should be a formal curricular offering that would fulfill certain course requirements needed for graduation. The internship program could meet the needs of various disciplines, such as the humanities, business, mathematics, or science.

Internship programs that are included as a component of the senior year experience and are credit-bearing may alleviate the need for additional staffing. Keep in mind, however, that these types of programs are a departure from the traditional educational experience that our schools have been conditioned to accept, so there will be some resistance and skepticism. The inclusion of these programs also has a profound impact on scheduling, so we need to discuss both of these concerns simultaneously.

Considering the success of the internship programs cited in this book, it is recommended that schools look toward block scheduling for senior classes. This would require that senior classes meet on alternate days for longer periods of time. This change will be met with resistance from teachers, parents, and administrators who have not yet fully embraced the importance of an internship program. However, this form of scheduling—while a radical departure from the academic culture in many schools—has significant benefits.

Anyone who has worked in a high school can identify the need to change the senior year experience. "Senioritis" strikes our oldest and most mature students at various times of the senior year, even as early as the beginning of September when they realize they have passed all of the standardized tests required for graduation and have taken the most challenging courses. It may strike sometime during the senior year when they receive their college acceptance letters. Whenever it hits, school officials, teachers, and parents begin to question how to channel the powerful energy of adolescence to help them move toward young adulthood.

The implementation of block scheduling will provide the opportunity for students to take the classes required to fulfill graduation requirements. If students also must complete a mandated research symposium and an internship program, they will be provided with a challenging and unique senior year that will position them well to take their next steps.

Scheduling of Classes

Block scheduling addresses the needs of the entire academic community on many fronts. First and foremost, it changes the educational experience of the student in their senior year of high school. Currently in many schools, senior classes meet every day and the academic paradigm changes very little from previous years. Although the curriculum does change and there are more elective and "college like" activities facilitated by the instructors, the entire academic community struggles with the challenges of adequately addressing the needs of senior year students. Whether it be a decline in academic focus, class cutting, or general apathy, there is a problem. The lives of many of these students have changed. Many are working after school, some are involved in a serious relationship, and many are participating in demanding, competitive extracurricular activities. Completing their homework on Tuesday morning for an economics class may not be high on their priority list.

Block scheduling provides the students with an opportunity to participate in coursework that is more aligned with the postsecondary experience. Scheduling classes on alternative days, mandating extensive reading of texts, and incorporating independent research will prepare the high school senior for the challenges that lie ahead. School officials need to examine how they can accomplish this radical departure from traditional education in their schools. It will be challenging to meet the needs of the students and offer a program that allows the students to choose the courses they want to take during their senior year of high school. The scheduling of advanced placement or special education classes also will be challenging. The scheduling gurus of your district need to sort out how to address the conflicts and the availability of certain "singleton" classes, or those with only one section, in order to meet the needs of the various groups of students.

The scheduling of classes on alternate days, or even twice a week, provides the opportunity and time for an effective and meaningful internship experience. Giving the students an opportunity to intern two full days per week in a well-structured work environment will make invaluable contributions to the individual growth of the individual. For example, consider a high school senior who wants to pursue a degree in elementary education in college. Twice a week, this high school senior could work with a master teacher in an elementary school and immerse themselves in the curriculum, instructional methodologies, and teaching strategies that will build a strong foundation to meet the demands of a postsecondary education program in elementary education. This experience will emulate the student teaching required to graduate from college and provide the student with an authentic and meaningful experience to reflect upon and make their undergraduate studies more meaningful. In addition, consider how this internship benefited the elementary students. They had an additional teaching assistant to help them address reading and math deficiencies, at no cost to the district. The senior class in any public high school has many students who possess this vision to become early childhood educators. We must ask the question: why aren't we utilizing these resources when everyone involved will benefit?

School districts need to look at the intricacies of their scheduling matrix and figure out how to weave the internship program into their schools. This is not an easy charge, but the entire academic community will benefit.

The Senior Year Research Component

Many districts currently require their seniors to conduct research and produce an extensive research paper for a specific course, usually in the humanities such as English or social studies. The teachers of high school seniors realize that this will be a requirement in postsecondary education, so valid attempts are made to prepare the graduating seniors for this future charge.

The implementation of block scheduling, along with an internship experience, provides the high school with the time, flexibility, and ability to emphasize the importance of independent research and advanced writing skills. When seniors return to high school after graduation to visit and socialize with their teachers, lack of preparation in this area is a common grievance that many of these college students voice. They cite their inability to meet this demand of their postsecondary experience. Unfortunately for these college freshman or sophomores, this demand only increases as students begin to choose their college major and look to prepare themselves for a career. The senior year experience should include activities of this nature that challenge these seniors academically, not to hinder their ability to graduate from high school or to negatively impact their grade point average, but to prepare them for the challenges that lie ahead in the postsecondary experience.

STUDENT RESPONSIBILITIES

The Senior Experience

The last year in high school needs to be evaluated by educational leaders. The way in which public educators treat their oldest, most experienced students has changed little over the past thirty years. These young adults are standing on the threshold of their future, looking at one of the most important and stressful transitions of their life. Secondary schools need to provide these students with opportunities to continue to grow, to accept more responsibility, and to become more independent learners. The "senior experience" needs to include activities that will provide individuals with the tools they need to make a seamless transition to college success.

Seniors in high school also need to view their last year in high school through a different lens. A majority of the students have already met the necessary requirements set forth by state education departments. For example, in New York state all of the mandated state tests are completed by the end of the junior year, with the exception of advanced mathematics and physics, which may be required for an "advanced designation" on their Regents diploma. Additionally, a percentage of seniors take rigorous Advanced Placement (AP) courses, which have been developed by the College Board. With the exception of these courses, however, students are merely completing coursework to accumulate the necessary credits required for graduation.

In less than one year, however, the students will be entering the competitive and challenging world of postsecondary education. High school seniors need to embrace different challenges during their senior year of high school. The inclusion of challenging academic coursework structured similar to college-level work, extensive work in research and writing, along with a unique internship experience that allows them to engage with the adult world will prepare the graduating senior for the challenges that lie ahead. Secondary educators need to place more responsibility on the shoulders of their oldest and wisest while they still have the support systems of their home and high school community. These challenges need to be embraced by the students, and we need to constantly remind them of the value of their "senior experience."

School leaders and educators need to look at what will be best for their students and engage in long-range strategic planning to enhance the senior experience. It is vital that the students also be included in this decision-making process and that their input is seriously considered. Educational reform of this nature needs to be embraced by all, especially the students themselves.

Internship Programs

The internship experience will provide the opportunity for students to step beyond the walls of their high school and engage in learning in a real-life situation. The stories told in this text support the fact that the internship experience promotes independence, personal accomplishment, a true passion, a unique experience, an enhanced work ethic, mature and adult relationships, success in college, and the experiences and tools they need to begin sorting out career options.

The internship experience needs to be close to the heart of the student, challenging and unique. The stories from this text highlighted the experiences of students who found strength and personal growth through their experiences and the impact that these experiences had regarding success in postsecondary education. It is vital that each student embrace and understand the importance of an internship opportunity.

Students need to look at internship opportunities toward the end of their junior year of high school. Districts need to set up parameters and guidelines for the students and building level mentors to ensure that the student's choice of an internship experience is a sound decision. Building level mentors, or advisors, need to engage in ongoing conversations with students to ensure that the student is pursuing a passion, not just a fleeting thought or idea. Students need to understand that the careful selection of their internship experience is vital to the success of the program.

Schools must help students understand that our society provides a plethora of internship opportunities, including education, finance, politics, entrepreneurship, medicine, advocacy groups, small business, philanthropy, and various community services. Through the revision of the "senior experience" to include block scheduling, the students will be able to make a commitment to their internship program and still juggle the demands of their extracurricular activities. In order for high school seniors to benefit from their "senior experience," their personal commitment is vital.

The Student/Mentor Relationship

All of the students who were interviewed in this text placed great value on the adult-student relationships that were fostered throughout their internship experience. All of the literature presented earlier in this text reinforces the need for students to transition from their adolescent world to the adult world. The internship experience will allow these young adults to flourish and grow in a structured, organized, demanding, and personal learning experience outside of the walls of their high school.

High schools must set up a protocol to have school-based mentors available to work with students during their internship experience. These mentors are usually chosen by the student due to the close and special relationship they have developed with the staff member during their tenure in high school. The role of these mentors varies from district to district; some are merely in an advisory role and are a sounding board for the student to reflect on their experiences during their internship. Other districts place a higher expectation on the mentor, to monitor academic progress and ensure that the student is meeting the requirements of the program. In many cases, the teachers involved in the "senior experience" program will be called upon to assist at the building level. The establishment of an effective protocol is vital to the success of the program.

The second mentor involved in the internship is the workplace mentor. This individual should be approached by the student and must be willing to follow all of the requirements of the program. In return, the mentor will receive hours of manpower in the form of an enthusiastic, committed, and passionate student intern. This relationship also needs to be fostered by both the student and the mentor over the course of the internship experience. Mutual respect and commitment are vital to this relationship and to the overall effectiveness of the internship experience.

All of the students interviewed in this research established a special relationship with the mentors they worked with during their internship. The workplace mentors, ranging from the local volunteer fire chief to a research scientist to a public advocate promoting the rights of gay and lesbian youth, made the student's internship experience special. Additionally, several of the students placed an importance on their school-based mentors or advisors who provided them with a "safe place" from which to pursue their dreams while still rooted in the familiar surroundings of their high school.

Internship programs need to place responsibility on the student and allow them to make personal and meaningful decisions. This departure from traditional schooling may be uncomfortable for many. But keep in mind that in less than one year they will need to make decisions of this nature, build relationships with adults and peers in the unfamiliar setting of a college campus, and perform academically without all of the supports of their home and high school. We will now briefly discuss the responsibilities of the postsecondary institution in the stressful and challenging transition to college and the continuance of internship opportunities at the postsecondary level.

THE ROLE OF POSTSECONDARY INSTITUTIONS

College Acceptance

After completing the junior year of high school, students are faced with many tasks to advance to the college of their choice. The application process from university to university may vary to some degree. But if you were to look at the common application used by many postsecondary institutions, the favorable attributes of an incoming freshman are clearly outlined by the required tasks on the application.

After speaking to several directors of guidance in public schools, the bottom line regarding the acceptance of students by a postsecondary institution is academic achievement in high school and the student's performance on the SAT or ACT standardized college admission tests. This has been the common practice of universities and colleges for many years, and it clearly makes sense if college success was solely based on academic performance. Studies have shown, however, that success in college is dependent upon many variables, only one of which is academic performance.

If we were to look at the salient portions of the common application, there is a section where the students are asked to provide information regarding their extracurricular, personal, and volunteer activities. Additionally, they are asked to write several short answer responses and a personal essay regarding other aspects of their life to provide the reviewer with additional information. It is obviously important for the admissions officers to see the total child.

It is unfortunate, however, that these portions of the application follow the request for the student to enter their academic achievement in high school as well as their performance on standardized tests. High school counselors also are well schooled in the requirements of postsecondary institutions. Colleges and universities are categorized by the selective nature of their institution and seek students with a certain level of academic success. Some may argue that it is the correct way to sort and evaluate students and that their academic performance should be the first and foremost determining factor to college acceptance.

The research of Tinto and Astin cite the importance of academic performance in high school as a determinant of success in college. They note, however, that many other attributes of the individual are essential. The ability of the student to have a successful college experience is dependent on many variables: their ability to meet the institution's academic demands, the individual's ability to make a successful transition, social adjustment, time management, coping with a new sense of independence, and the development of one's autonomy. Collectively or independently, these are the factors that determine whether or not an individual is successful in college.

Postsecondary institutions need to examine the overall experiences of the child as a determining factor in the admissions process. Internships are one of these experiences that need to be seriously considered by universities.

Subjective versus Objective Selection Criteria

After reviewing and reading the findings in this text, the need of institutions to measure the readiness of prospective students by meaningful yardsticks is apparent. The attributes fostered through the internship experience clearly provide the individual with the foundation to be successful in college. These qualities, however, are subjective in nature. Protocol can be established quite easily to look at prospective students objectively using academic performance as the primary focus. These protocols have been established and used for years with the same results regarding student attrition and failure in postsecondary education.

In order to develop a protocol that weighs both objective and subjective data in the college acceptance process, postsecondary institutions need to reflect upon their admission process and determine the qualities required for a student to be successful and meet the academic demands of their institution. If they are using the common application, greater importance needs to be placed on pages three and four, where the student is offered the opportunity to personalize the application and cite attributes overlooked by standardized tests. This is a challenging charge for postsecondary institutions, but change is needed.

Once the student has been accepted and arrives at their postsecondary institution, colleges and universities understand the need to assist students in the transition from high school to college and have made earnest fiscal and personnel commitments to these efforts.

Transition Strategies and Internship Opportunities

Earlier in the text, transition strategies from several universities were discussed. We discussed the transition strategies of a wide variety of universities, including the highly selective Princeton University, the large University of Maryland, and the small college in the New York State University system, Cortland. All of these postsecondary institutions recognize the need to assist incoming freshman at this time of their academic career and have made meaningful efforts to help each student.

Earlier in this text we discussed the findings of Tinto, who based his research in the field of anthropology and the student's ability to change membership and become a part of a new community. College freshman are placed into an unfamiliar place with people whom they do not know and are suddenly living and working alongside. They have left the safety of their home, high school, and lifelong friends. These factors clearly affect the student's ability to be successful in college. Students who are recruited for specific activities, such as athletics or performing arts, are immediately involved with other students and given a common charge. There are also opportunities for students to participate in many clubs similar to those established experiences in high school. However, universities need to ensure that all students have a life outside of the classroom.

Student involvement in internship programs while in college will allow the student to stay connected with the real world. Postsecondary institutions need to understand the value of diverse experiences while in college, and many of them do. The inclusion of internships and studying abroad are common in many universities, and student involvement in these programs needs to be emphasized, if not required. The endless energy, insight, and intellectual attributes of these young adults need to be nurtured through programs of this nature as soon as students enroll in college. This also will help address the dropout phenomenon and allow individual students to stay connected with their university, rather than wandering through an unfamiliar place with little or no direction.

NOTES

1. H. R. Clinton, *It Takes a Village: And Other Lessons Children Teach Us* (New York: Simon and Schuster, 1996).
2. Clinton, *It Takes a Village*, 266.
3. C. M. Engstrom and V. Tinto, "Working Together for Service Learning," *About Campus* (July–August 1997): 10.
4. Willard R. Daggett, "Achieving Academic Excellence through Rigor and Relevance," International Center for Leadership in Education, 2005.

FINAL THOUGHTS

It was the intention of this text to look at the needs of high school students as they pass through the challenging years of adolescence to becoming an adult. These years are difficult to figure out; all you need to do is ask the parent of a high school student. There is compelling research about the nature of the adolescent world and how at times it can constrain the child from reaching their potential. This adolescent world will continue to exist, and many aspects of it are developmentally beneficial to the child. However, there comes a time when students need to be challenged and prepare for the difficult transition to postsecondary education. The college departure phenomenon is a fact, and it compels us to examine the experiences we are offering our children in our public schools and change the status quo where necessary, especially during the senior year of high school.

The students who provided us with genuine, authentic reflections of their experiences in high school valued their internship programs. The impact of their real-world learning experience has stayed with them for many years, and they felt strongly that it made invaluable contributions to their college success and personal growth. Educators, parents, and students need to effectively collaborate and plan to incorporate experiential learning experiences into the high school curriculum. All will benefit.

Appendix

ACHIEVING ACADEMIC EXCELLENCE THROUGH RIGOR AND RELEVANCE

Willard R. Daggett

WHAT DEFINES ACADEMIC EXCELLENCE?

The changing nature of work, technology, and competition in the global job market has far outpaced what the U.S. education system provides for students, despite the ongoing efforts of educators and communities to improve their schools. Priorities and goals set by educators at all levels of academia are not closing the gap. The focus on state assessments as the one true measure of academic excellence is slowly but surely limiting our young people's chances of experiencing any semblance of the success in life that we expect for them and that they believe school will provide for them.

The present structure of the education system does students a tremendous injustice by not delivering the quality schooling we are capable of. State assessments play a role in education, but a score on a test will not help the student when he or she is competing for a job with someone from China or India. What is important is that

---

Used with permission of the International Center for Leadership in Education (see www.LeaderEd.com).

students enter the global economy with the ability to apply what they learned in school to a variety of ever-changing situations that they couldn't foresee before graduating. That is the mark of a quality education and a truer indication of academic excellence.

Since the publication of *A Nation at Risk* in 1983, U.S. schools have experienced increasing pressure from government and business leaders to raise academic standards for all students. More recently, the *No Child Left Behind* (NCLB) legislation has caused states to take a serious look at their standards and assessment programs. Widespread changes in these programs are occurring nationwide in order to comply with the adequate yearly progress (AYP) provision of NCLB. Every district, school, superintendent, principal, and teacher in this country is feeling pressure to get all students to minimum proficiency levels.

While having all students achieve academic proficiency is a worthy goal, it should be only the starting line. State assessments have become so "high-stakes" that classroom instruction is geared toward the sole purpose of passing them. In this respect, state assessments have become the finish line. The student's ability to apply high-rigor knowledge in a relevant, real-world setting needs to be the true finish line; instead, it has become an afterthought.

Traditionally, instructional planning was divided into three components: curriculum, instruction, and assessment. In too many schools, these components are approached as three separate, sequential steps, with assessment being the finish line. In the 1990s, state standards entered into the equation as a fourth component. A rigorous and relevant education is a product of effective learning, which takes place when standards, curriculum, instruction, and assessment interrelate and reinforce each other. The value of state assessments is undeniable, but we cannot view them as the definition of academic excellence. Unfortunately, many of those in education do. When assessment is viewed as the end goal or finish line, the test itself becomes a barrier to high levels of student achievement. However, if curriculum, instruction, and relevant learning become the focus, the tests will take care of themselves.

Globalization and rapid technological advancements are having dramatic effects on the ways we communicate and conduct business as well as in our personal lives. Education should increase students' understanding of the world around them. Unfortunately, there is little or no connectivity or integration between subjects and grades in most U.S. schools. As students move from class to class and progress to the next grade, they are exposed to isolated bits of content-specific knowledge, but they are not taught how what they learn in one class relates to another or its application in the world outside of school.

Incorporating more rigorous and relevant instruction in classrooms is a realistic goal and will yield immediate results in students' enthusiasm to learn. When students are engaged in the learning process, real achievement takes place, and their chances to excel at what they do increase. Often, all that is required is a change of attitude and the willingness to restructure education so that it prepares students for life, not just the state test or for more school. Effectively integrating subjects is an important step . . . and it costs little.

RIGOR/RELEVANCE FRAMEWORK

Studies have shown that students understand and retain knowledge best when they have applied it in a practical, relevant setting. A teacher who relies on lecturing does not provide students with optimal learning opportunities. Instead, students go to school to watch the teacher work. The International Center's Rigor/Relevance Framework is a powerful tool that has captured the imagination of teachers to aspire to teach students to high rigor and high relevance.

All educators can use the Rigor/Relevance Framework to set their own standards of excellence as well as to plan the objectives

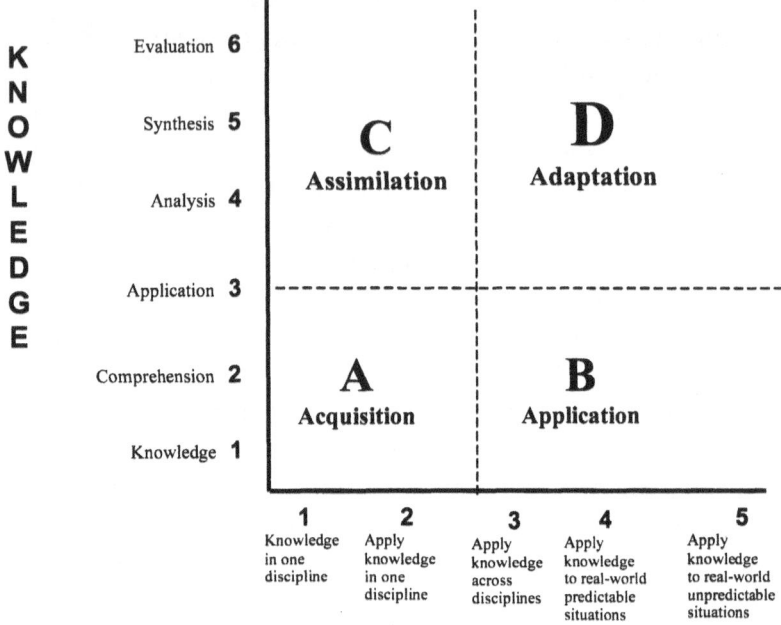

they wish to achieve. This versatile Framework applies to standards, curriculum, instruction, and assessment.

When planning a lesson using the Rigor/Relevance Framework, it is important to maintain a consistent level of rigor and relevance. For example, if a teacher has lofty curriculum objectives in Quadrant D but develops instruction and test questions that are in Quadrant A, it is unlikely that students will reach the teacher's high expectations. Similarly, if a teacher designs high-rigor instructional activities but uses a low-rigor assessment tool, the test will not be an accurate measure of what students have learned.

When implementing the Rigor/Relevance Framework in a classroom, school, district, or state, it is of great importance to design instruction and develop assessments that measure Quadrant D skills. This enables students not only to gain knowledge, but also to develop skills such as inquiry, investigation, and experimentation.

In thinking about ways to incorporate the Rigor/Relevance Framework in instruction and assessment, it is helpful to consider the roles that students and teachers take. When instruction and expected student learning is in Quadrant A, the focus is on *teacher work*. Teachers expend energy to create and assess learning activities—providing lesson content, creating worksheets, and grading student work. In this scenario the student becomes a passive learner.

When instruction and expected learning moves to Quadrant B, the emphasis is on the *student* doing real-world *work*. This work involves more real-world tasks than Quadrant A and generally takes more time for students to complete.

When instruction and expected learning falls in Quadrant C, the *student* is required to *think* in complex ways—to analyze, compare, create, and evaluate. Traditionally, this has been the level of learning that students graduated from high school with.

Quadrant D learning requires the *student* to *think and work*. Roles have shifted from teacher-centered instruction in Quadrant A to student-centered learning. Quadrant D requires that students understand the standard or benchmark being taught thoroughly, but equally important, they must also understand and conceptualize relevant applications for the content being covered.

ROLE OF ASSESSMENT AT STATE AND LOCAL LEVELS

Quadrant D implies high rigor and relevance, but this is not to be confused with a high level of difficulty. In fact, there are basic Quadrant A concepts that, in reality, are quite complex. Quadrant A concepts are taught in isolation, though. For example, mitosis— the "entire sequence of processes in cell division in which the diploid number of chromosomes is retained in both daughter cells" (*Webster's II New College Dictionary*, 1995)—is a challenging concept for many people. However, it falls in Quadrant A because it merely requires understanding in one discipline.

During my presentations, I ask audiences if they know what a "blastocyst" is. The vast majority do not. A blastocyst is a stage of development of an embryo when it is around five days old and made up of about one hundred cells. One must have a thorough understanding of this single but very complex concept, along with many other individual but similarly complex concepts, in order to enter the stem cell debate.

Quadrant A content is taught in isolation. Quadrants B and D give that content meaning and application. Students cannot perform at Quadrant B and D levels without first mastering Quadrant A skills and knowledge through the learning process. Debating one side for or against embryonic stem cell research is a classic Quadrant D activity because it requires that the debater develop a rigorous knowledge base to argue an issue that people of different backgrounds care very strongly about.

Designing local or state assessments at the various grade levels presents unique challenges. Designing the right assessment at all levels is essential to helping students achieve the desired level of rigor and relevance. To maximize student learning, it is important to identify the objectives of the learning experience prior to planning instruction and assessment. Assessments should be selected to match the desired level of rigor and relevance.

At the local level, performance-based assessments are an effective way for teachers to monitor whether students are able to understand the content and apply their knowledge. Well-constructed performance tasks help the teacher and students know if they really understand the material or if they are merely following a pattern they have learned for regurgitating information they have memorized. Students become better problem solvers when they are given the opportunity to find original solutions to problems and reflect on what worked and what did not.

RIGOR AND RELEVANCE IN STATE ASSESSMENTS

State departments of education have the great but difficult responsibility to create fair and comprehensive assessments of the curricular content covered leading up to the state test. This was a difficult job before AYP. The compounded pressure of getting all students to attain minimum proficiency on state tests has begun to reveal some alarming trends.

State assessments are the most difficult aspect of K–12 education in which to incorporate both rigor and relevance. There are a number of reasons why this is so.

State Tests Need to Be Easy to Score

In any state, the sheer number of students being tested and the vast array of standards and benchmarks to be assessed require that the exams be scored with expedience. Multiple-choice questions lend themselves to efficient scoring and are the most commonly used way to assess students' knowledge. With multiple-choice questions, the correct answer is always shown and the student needs only to choose wisely.

Multiple-choice questions, and therefore state assessments, tend to be predominantly Quadrant A based. Quadrant D-based questions take longer for students to answer and evaluators to grade. There is also the challenge of scoring the work objectively and fairly for all students in the state.

Content Tested in Isolation

State assessments test knowledge in one discipline, which lends itself to Quadrant A-based instruction and learning. To be in Quadrants B and D, learning must be interdisciplinary. With high-stakes state assessments, many teachers are inclined to identify the content in their subject area that is likely to be tested and teach to the test.

Educators and the public must recognize that it is often not feasible for state testing programs to test at high levels of rigor and relevance. Therefore, academic excellence cannot be defined by passing the state test, but rather hinges on the teaching and learning students experience throughout their entire education process. Educators who value a rigorous and relevant education for all students view the perception of the state assessments as the finish line as a great impediment to academic excellence. Only when people change their mind-set can schools get their priorities in order.

Cultural Bias

State testing programs are under the microscope. With so many people with different views, values, and agendas paying close attention to what is on the test, test developers feel like they are walking a tightrope. So even though they may want to incorporate more relevant text passages and test questions in the assessments, developers are wary of presenting any content that might label the test or themselves as biased for or against a certain group.

Quadrant D, real-world test components are exposed to this sort of criticism. As in all things in life, what is relevant to some is not always relevant to others; state tests, first and foremost, need to be fair.

Whether consciously or not, state assessment programs test primarily in Quadrant A. Data collected by the International Center illuminates the status of rigor and relevance on state tests. Though it is difficult and costly to develop state assessments that are predominantly Quadrant D-based, it is critical that state leaders set targets to reach the maximum levels of rigor and relevance they are able to test.

By specifying targets for rigor and relevance in each assessment, a state education department can convey this information to schools and districts. State leadership could also inform teachers why, for the reasons identified above, it is not always feasible to test for high rigor and relevance on state tests and that they should set expectations for rigor and relevance in instruction and local assessments that exceed those of the state tests. This will not diminish the importance of tests, but rather place them in the proper perspective by emphasizing effective learning and instruction.

State tests should not be perceived as a tool for measuring everything that a student needs to know and be able to do before moving on to the next grade, an institution of higher education, or a career. Teachers should be inspired to be the ones who define academic excellence through a rigorous and relevant education and not delegate that responsibility to the state testing programs.

EMPHASIS ON EFFECTIVE INSTRUCTION

In the U.S. education system, the most effective learning occurs in the elementary grades. Elementary teachers are not hindered by subject boundaries as much as in later grades, so interdisciplinary instruction occurs more naturally. Elementary teachers spend more time throughout the day with their students, and that interaction allows for easier and more plentiful teaching opportunities than occur in later grades. Elementary students are uninhibited in their enthusiasm to learn and not afraid to ask questions. Many teachers would agree that the most effective means of teaching is answering students' questions because they are showing interest in the subject and will remember the answer.

By the time students get to high school, instruction becomes segmented, and many students become less engaged in the learning process. Their ability to investigate interconnections between what they learn is stifled because the teacher has too much material to cover and not enough time.

Students cannot attain a Quadrant D-level education one subject at a time. We need to allow students to explore for themselves the relevance of what they are learning.

At the high school level, career and technical education programs provide the most effective learning opportunities. Not only are students applying skills and knowledge to real-world situations in their CTE programs, but also they are drawing on knowledge learned in their core subjects. Students who participate in CTE programs should be well prepared for state exams because the academics they learn are used in Quadrants B and D. The key is to tie those academics to core content areas. In this respect, CTE teachers can be a great help to language arts, math, and science teachers by reinforcing the skills and concepts that students learn in those subjects.

The lecture approach to instruction, still so prevalent in high schools, supports students with Quadrants A and C learning styles, so these students tend to do better than Quadrants B and D learners under the present structure. Teachers who prefer the instructional strategy of lecturing are usually Quadrants A and C learners themselves.

The difference among the four quadrants of the Rigor/Relevance Framework in terms of academic complexity really relates to students' aptitudes, interests, and learning styles. In many cases, students who are quick to master theories (A/C) will struggle with applications (B/D) unless they are properly contextualized. Conversely, some students intuitively understand how to apply knowledge to a situation but have trouble understanding the basic theory behind it. These students may be very bright, but they have trouble exhibiting that on the state tests because the assessments are not designed with their learning styles and aptitudes in mind.

If the rigor and relevance of Quadrants B and D became the predominant instructional practice, all students will benefit. Students with Quadrants A and C learning styles and aptitudes would be challenged to develop skills they will need to compete in the global job market. Although they may be great students and score well on tests, many are not prepared for success in the workforce. Students with Quadrants B and D learning styles would finally get a chance to shine. With proper instruction, these students will understand the theory behind what they are learning. All students benefit because they will be challenged to achieve academic excellence, which ultimately boils down to applying rigorous knowledge to unpredictable, real-world situations, such as those that drive our rapidly changing world . . . and the tests will take care of themselves.

BIBLIOGRAPHY

Abramson, T., and V. Leviatin. 1980. *Woodlands Individualized Senior Experience Manual.* Greenburgh, NY: Greenburgh Central School District No. 7.

Astin, A. 1975. *Preventing Students from Dropping Out.* San Francisco: Jossey-Bass.

———. 1977. *Four Critical Years.* San Francisco: Jossey-Bass.

———. 1993. *What Matters in College? Four Critical Years Revisited.* San Francisco: Jossey-Bass.

Auerbach, C., and L. Silverstein. 2003. *Qualitative Data: An Introduction to Coding and Analysis.* New York: New York University Press.

Bancroft, A., and S. Rogers. 2004. "Emile Durkheim—The Work." Introduction to Social Theory: Social Theory On-Line. Retrieved January 28, 2004, from www.cf.ac.uk/socsi/undergraduate/introsoc/durkheim.html.

———. 2004. "Max Weber—The Work." Introduction to Social Theory: Social Theory On-Line. Retrieved January 28, 2004, from www.cf.ac.uk/socsi/undergraduate/introsoc/webrwrk.html.

Berger, J., and J. Braxton. 1998. "Revising Tinto's Interactionist Theory of Student Departure through Theory Elaboration: Examining the Role of Organizational Attributes in the Persistence Process." *Research in Higher Education* 39, no. 2:103–19.

Bloom, B. 1956. *Taxonomy of Educational Objectives: The Classification of Educational Goals*. New York: David McKay.
Borg, W., M. Gall, and J. Gall. 2003. *Educational Research: An Introduction*. Boston: Allyn & Bacon.
Borman, K., P. Cookson, A. Sadovnik, and J. Spade. 1996. *Implementing Educational Reform: Sociological Perspectives on Education*. Norwood, NJ: Ablex.
Bradley, M. 2002. *Yes, Your Teen Is Crazy*. Gig Harbor, WA: Harbor.
Braxton, J. 2000. *Reworking the Student Departure Puzzle*. Nashville, TN: Vanderbilt University Press.
Bridges, W. 1991. *Managing Transitions*. Cambridge, MA: Perseus.
Callahan, R. 1962. *Education and the Cult of Efficiency*. Chicago: University of Chicago Press.
Cantor, N. F. 1999. *The Encyclopedia of the Middle Ages*. New York: Penguin.
Clinton, H. R. 1996. *It Takes a Village: And Other Lessons Children Teach Us*. New York: Simon and Schuster.
Coleman, J. 1961. *The Adolescent Society*. New York: Glencoe.
Cusick, P. 1973. *Inside High School: The Student's World*. New York: Holt, Reinhart, Winston.
———. 1992. *The Educational System: Its Nature and Logic*. New York: McGraw Hill.
Daggett, W. R. 2005. "Achieving Academic Excellence through Rigor and Relevance." International Center for Leadership in Education. Retrieved November 1, 2007, from www.leadered.com/pdf/Academic_Excellence.pdf.
Darder, A. 2002. *Reinventing Paulo Freire*. Boulder, CO: Westview.
Dewey, J. 1944. *Democracy and Education*. New York: The Free Press.
———. 1958. *Philosophy of Education*. Totowa, NJ: Littlefield, Adams.
———. 1966. *Lectures in the Philosophy of Education, 1899*. New York: Random House.
Educational Research Service. 2003. *K–12 Principals' Guide to No Child Left Behind*. Arlington, VA: Educational Research Service.
Elkins, S. A., J. M. Braxton, and G. W. James. 2000. "Tinto's Separation Stage and Its Influence on First-Semester College Student Persistence." *Research in Higher Education* 41, no. 2:251–67.

BIBLIOGRAPHY

Ellett, T. E. 2005. *Building Engagement in Urban Universities: A Student Perspective on Residential Learning Communities*. PhD diss. New York: Fordham University.

Engel, M. 2000. *The Struggle for Control of Public Education: Market Ideology vs. Democratic Values*. Philadelphia: Temple University Press.

Engstrom, C. M., and V. Tinto. 1997. "Working Together for Service Learning." *About Campus* (July–August): 10–15.

Freire, P. 1994. *Pedagogy of Hope*. New York: Continuum.

Glasser, W. 1990. *The Quality School: Managing Students without Coercion*. New York: HarperCollins.

Green, L. 2001. *Communication, Technology and Society*. London: Sage.

Hirsch, E. D., Jr. 1996. *The Schools We Need: Why We Don't Have Them*. New York: Doubleday.

Hoffman, L. M. 2002. "Why High Schools Don't Change: What Students and Their Yearbooks Tell Us." *High School Journal* 86, no. 2:22–37. Retrieved on December 9, 2005, from www.fordham.edu. Ebsco host research databases.

Howard, P., and S. Jones. 2004. *Society Online: The Internet in Context*. Thousand Oaks, CA: Sage.

Institute for American Values. 2003. *Hardwired to Connect: The New Scientific Case for Authoritative Communities*. New York: Institute for American Values.

Johnson, J., V. Dupuis, D. Musial, G. Hall, and D. Gollnick. 2002. *Introduction to the Foundations of American Education*. Boston: Allyn & Bacon.

Kirst, M., and A. Venezia. 2004. *From High School to College: Improving Opportunities for Success in Postsecondary Education*. San Francisco: Jossey-Bass.

Littky, D., and S. Grabelle. 2004. *The Big Picture: Education is Everyone's Business*. Alexandria, VA: Association for Supervision and Curriculum Development (ASCD).

Mortimer, J., and R. Larson. 2002. *The Changing Adolescent Experience: Societal Trends and the Transition to Adulthood*. New York: Cambridge University Press.

New York State Education Department (N.Y.S.E.D.). 2005. "General Education and Diploma Requirements." Retrieved September 2, 2005, from http://www.emsc.nysed.gov/part100/pages/diprequire.pdf.

Noddings, N. 1992. *The Challenge to Care in Schools*. New York: The Teachers College Press.

Orfield, G., and M. Kornhaber. 2001. *Raising Standards or Raising Barriers*. New York: Century Foundation.

Organisation for Economic Co-operation and Development (OECD). 1983. *Education and Work: The Views of the Young*. Paris: OECD.

Paige, R. 2003. *No Child Left Behind: A Parents Guide*. Washington, DC: Education Publications Center.

Plato. 1986. *The Republic*. Buffalo, NY: Prometheus.

Princeton Freshman Seminars. 2004–2005. "Introduction to the Program of Freshman Seminars in the Residential Colleges." Retrieved January 24, 2005, from http://www.princeton.edu/pr/pub/fs/04/01.html.

Rogers, C. R. 1969. *Freedom to Learn*. Columbus, OH: Merrill.

Rogers, C. R., and H. Freiberg. 1994. *Freedom to Learn*. Columbus, OH: Merrill.

Rousseau, J. J. 1969. *Emile*. London: Aldine.

Sax, G. 1968. *Empirical Foundations of Educational Research*. Englewood Cliffs, NJ: Prentice-Hall.

Schwebel, M. 2003. *Remaking America's Three School Systems*. Lanham, MD: Scarecrow.

Seidman, A. 2005. *College Student Retention*. Westport, CT: Praeger.

Spring, J. 2000. *The Universal Right to Education*. Mahwah, NJ: Lawrence Erlbaum.

Steinberg, A. 1998. *Real Learning, Real Work*. New York: Routledge.

Steinberg, A., K. Cushman, and R. Riordan. 1999. *Schooling for the Real World: The Essential Guide to Rigorous and Relevant Learning*. San Francisco: Jossey-Bass.

Stern, D. 2001. "Career Academies and High School Reform Before, During, and After the School-to-Work Movement. Spotlight on Student Success." Washington, DC: Office of Educational Research and Improvement. Retrieved November 14, 2007, from http://www.temple.edu/LSS/pdf/spotlights/600/spot606.pdf.

SUNY Cortland. 2004. "COR 101: The Cortland Experience." Retrieved December 12, 2004, from http://www.cortland.edu/advisement/COR101/index.html.

Teare, C. 2005. "Cut Senior Year in Half," *Education Week* 25, no. 6:32.

Tinto, V. 1993 [1987]. *Leaving College: Rethinking the Causes and Cures of Student Attrition*. Chicago: University of Chicago Press.

Tinto, V., and A. Goodsell-Love. 1993. "Building Community." *Liberal Education* 79, no. 4:0024–1822. Retrieved July 8, 2005, from http://web32.epnet.com.avoserv.library.fordham.edu.

University of Maryland Orientation. 2004. "Univ Classes: New Student Seminars That Help You Achieve." Retrieved December 12, 2004, from http://www.orientation.umd.edu/univ/univ_1_welcome.html.

University of South Carolina. 2003. "International Conference on the First-Year Experience." Retrieved December 12, 2004, from http://www.sc.edu/fye/events/presentation/international2003/ppt/1.

———. 2005. "National Resource Center for the First-Year Experience." Retrieved December 10, 2005 from www.sc.edu/fye.

Vaughn, S., J. Schumm, and J. Sinagub. 1996. *Focus Group Interviews in Education and Psychology*. Thousand Oaks, CA: Sage.

Walter, G., and S. Marks. 1981. *Experiential Learning and Change*. New York: John Wiley.

Weber, M. 1968. *Max Weber on Law in Economy and Society*. New York: Simon and Schuster.

Webster's Unabridged Dictionary. 1983. New York: Simon and Schuster.

Whitehead, A. N. 1929. *The Aims of Education*. New York: The Free Press.

Yorktown Heights Fire Department (Y.H.F.D.). 2005. *Yorktown Heights Fire Department: Junior Corps Standard Operating Guidelines*. Yorktown Heights, NY: author.

ABOUT THE AUTHOR

Dr. Randall Glading has worked in public high schools for the past twenty-seven years. Because thousands of his students have experienced the "senior slump," he is committed to changing the status quo. He is currently a school administrator at Yorktown Central Schools in New York.

www.ingramcontent.com/pod-product-compliance
Lightning Source LLC
Chambersburg PA
CBHW031711230426
43668CB00006B/179